CONSUMER GUIDE®

CARS OF THE 50s

Automobiles Of The 1950s 4

At least a quarter million people are collecting old cars today, and many of them are fans of 1950s automobiles. These collectors feel that the '50s was an era marked by some of the most attractive styling the automotive world has ever seen, as well as many technological advances. Here's a guide to the most collectible cars of the '50s and year-by-year reports on all the models from the major auto makers of this extraordinary decade.

Numerous other automotive ventures marked the 1950s—little-known vehicles, one-offs and low-production cars. Though they may not have been built in great numbers, they're worth remembering as part of this exciting period in automobile history.

This edition published by:

Beekman House
A Division of Crown Publishers, Inc.
One Park Avenue
New York, N.Y. 10016
By arrangement with Publications International, Ltd.

Cover Design: Frank F. Peiler

Automobiles of the 1950s

Do you like to imagine that automobile tailfins really did "add stability at high speeds"? Do you wish you'd been able to enter the Mexican Road Race or take part in the Mobilgas Economy Run? Do you enjoy recalling PowerFlite, Turbo-Drive and Dyna-flow; and do you get turned on by thoughts of fuel-injected Chevys and hemi-head Chrysler 300s? Do you think that the departure of Hudson, Packard and Edsel from Detroit was a real shame—something akin to the Dodgers' departure from Brooklyn? If so, this book is for you.

Even if you don't consider yourself a fan of 1950s cars, you'll like CARS OF THE '50s. The automobiles discussed here are more than just vehicles with strange shapes and strange-sounding names. They're representatives of the art and technology of an important decade in American history.

The cars of the 1950s have their critics. According to some of them, these cars are what made the American transportation scene the "mess" it is today. Some say these cars were heavy, ungainly, dumb-looking beasts of burden with no redeeming virtues. Those who do not criticize the 1950s cars directly often do so indirectly by ignoring the decade altogether. The history of the automobile, they've said, is marked by dramatic experimentation through 1925, and by great progress from that year to 1950. They say nothing of technological advances between 1950 and 1960. That could be because the styling of these cars sometimes overshadows their engineering.

But there were some important automotive advances between '50 and '60. For instance, torsion-bar suspension, short-stroke V8s, efficient automatic transmissions, fuel injection and unit construction were introduced. The decade brought impressive progress in body design, including the hardtop, and the all-steel station wagon that was more car than truck.

If these years brought some of the worst styling excesses, they also were marked by some of the finest automotive designs of all time: the Studebaker "Loewy coupes," the Continental Mark IIs, the Darrin-styled Kaisers, the two-seat Thunderbirds. Finally—and this may come as a surprise—American cars of this decade are considered by many experts to have been safer than cars had ever been before. Maybe the seatbelts, padded dashes and sunken steering wheels of the '50s weren't merely sales gimmicks.

There are, conservatively speaking, a quarter million people collecting old cars today—up from a handful of eccentrics 10 years ago. The proportion of collectors dedicated to cars of the 1950s is probably the highest of any decade. Though nostalgia does influence them, their appreciation for imaginative new ideas embodied by so many different makes also plays a part.

There's something else about these automobiles that even their enthusiasts often fail to cite, probably because it's so universally accepted. The cars have an intrinsic character that the automobile industry somehow lost between 1960 and 1978. They were different—vastly different—from the cars of today. Theirs was probably the last full decade when a manufacturer dared sell a car that was clearly unique, like the "step-down" Hudson, the tiny Nash Metropolitan and the fiberglass Woodill Wildfire. They were also built differently. Cars of the '50s had interiors of comfortable mohair and genuine leather; bodies of heavy-gauge steel. Their makers shunned things like plastic, cardboard, decals and rubber bumpers. While the average family car of 1950-59 probably handled as sloppily as everyone says it did, it was also built with more pure integrity than its more nimble successors. Every piece of trim met every other piece of trim precisely where intended. Every door, trunk lid and hood closed with a resounding clunk, swinging shut on bank-vault hinges. Collectors still discover rust-free examples with six-figure mileage; their interiors, paint and mechanical components in approximately the same shape as when they left the factory a quarter century ago. What will a '78 car look like in 2003?

All these attributes give cars of the 1950s undeniable appeal. Since you can still drive them as you would a new car, they're even supplying a realistic alternative to today's models. To more than a few buyers, it makes more sense to spend $3000 for a Chrysler 300 that they can sell later at a profit than it does to spend $9000 for a '78 Chrysler that'll be worth $900 in a short time.

How To Buy, Where To Find It

What do you look for in a 1950s car today? If investment and speculation are not your goals, the answer is: nothing. Just pick the model that speaks your language. If you want one that will increase in value quickly, "character" becomes a factor. The cars of the '50s are loaded with it. The 1957-59 Ford Skyliner, with its retractable hardtop, is an innovative design that still turns heads now as it did 20 years ago. The early Studebaker Starlight coupes, with their wraparound backlights, are as attractive now as they were in 1950. The 1954 Kaiser Darrin, with its sliding doors, never fails to amaze people today. The 1955-56 Packards, with self-leveling torsion-bar suspension, were the ultimate in ride and handling among big cars. Had the same idea occurred to GM, we might still find it on the latest Cadillac Seville.

Unless you're a whiz at restorations, a car in original condition is a better investment than one that needs a lot of work. Overrestored cars can actually sell for less than good originals, and an authentic restoration can cost more than the car itself is worth.

Lately, collectors have recognized the value of cars with original paint jobs, interiors and engine compartments. It's easier now for such slightly imperfect cars to compete against restorations at *concours d'elegance.* Sometimes there are even special classes for them. The level of interest in originals is high at such shows—and enthusiasts usually swarm such a car taking pictures and exclaiming.

The ideal place to look for bargain originals is your hometown newspaper. Someone who bought the car new and has maintained it carefully ever since is inclined to be happier with a "good home" for it than a huge profit. (Occasionally, however, you may run into the owner who's convinced that what he has is worth a fortune.)

It's important too to subscribe to one of the three major sources of old-car advertising. These periodicals list huge quantities of cars, parts, literature and services.

Hemmings Motor News, P. O. Box 380, Bennington, VT 05201. Published monthly.
Cars & Parts, P. O. Box 299, Sesser, IL 62884. Published monthly.
Old Cars, Iola, WI 54945. Published weekly.

The 1950s phenomenon has been going on for a long time, however, so some models are better buys than others. Here we present a rundown of the most important companies, with notes on the standing of their products among collectors today—especially the models that are particular bargains at present.

American Motors. Including for this purpose the Hudsons and Nashes built prior to the creation of AMC in 1954, we find wide differences in popularity. The NASCAR-champion Hudson Hornets have certainly been discovered, while the Nash is the most ignored marque in the postwar field. Still, there are many worthwhile buys within each make.

The Hudson Wasp, for example, is much less expensive than the Hornet on today's market. Having a shorter wheelbase and smaller engine, it doesn't pack the Hornet's punch. But it provides the same durability, it rides and handles well for a car of its size, and is surprisingly easy on gas.

The little Hudson Jet is also generally overlooked. *Road & Track* found it the best compact of all in 1953, and it's even attractive compared to compacts today. With the same amount of money and a little time to look, you can find a low-mileage, rust-free, original Jet that is livelier than and just as economical as a 1970s compact. Like all collector cars, it will gain instead of lose value.

The problem Nashes have is their susceptibility to rust. For this reason, there aren't many of them left. Low demand, however, results in ridiculously low prices. A desirable 1954 Ambassador Country Club hardtop equipped with the 140-horsepower Le Mans engine recently changed hands for $1500. It had 32,000 original miles and was nearly undetectable from new. Metropolitans are more popular. Ramblers are less so, but one day collectors will sense the value of the first modern compact and will start gathering them in.

Chrysler Corporation. For years, collector interest here has surrounded the wood-embellished Town & Country and high-performance Chrysler 300. The former was built mainly in the 1940s, and its price has skyrocketed over the last several years, suggesting that other Chryslers may be good investments. "Letter series" Chrysler 300s do not yet bring the five-figure prices of Town & Countrys, but they're not cheap either. Limited-edition performance models like the Plymouth Fury, Dodge D-500 and De Soto Adventurer now command upwards of $3000 for prime originals, though even at that price they're good investments with appreciation potential.

The real bulk of 1950-59 Chrysler production is available, reasonably priced, with lots of variety. The 1950-52 period gave us the winsome Dodge Wayfarer convertible, for example. It is still a good buy, usually priced at less than $2000. All Chryslers, De Sotos, Dodges and Plymouths of 1950-54 are solid, reliable, economical cars. The number of low-mileage examples appearing is great. In a recent issue of *Hemmings Motor News,* we counted no fewer than 34 such cars with less than 40,000 miles on their odometers. While the occasional owner tests P.T. Barnum's theory with a $6000 price tag, you can buy one for less than half that much.

Chrysler products became increasingly gaudy and rust-prone in the late '50s, years that seem to be overlooked except by collectors of 300s. The 1955-57 period seems better than the 1958-60 period now. The '55 Dodge Custom Royals, for example, are still nice-looking and offer a great deal of power from the economical Six or D-500 V8s. The 1957-58 Plymouths sported some of the best styling of those two years. They were fast, and torsion-bar front suspension gave them good handling. Imperials of 1955-56 are elegant cars that are soundly built, though they are not economical to run. Imperial prices have lagged behind those of Cadillacs from the same years, making the Imperials better buys, but perhaps not as good for in-

Automobiles of the 1950s

vestment as the GM luxury car.

There are plenty of low-production Chrysler products worth considering, if you find one. The luxurious Coronado of 1955 and the Pacesetter convertible of 1956 are two from De Soto. Plymouth's top-line 1959 Sport Fury is fairly rare, and the low-production Exner-Ghia specials are extremely so. Yet all but the Exner-Ghias are not excessively priced at present. Convertibles from Chrysler, like those from other manufacturers, are the rarest and are the most sought-after.

Ford. Dealing with the long-established collector's items first, the Continental Mark II and two-seat Thunderbirds in fine condition began to sell for $10,000 and up long ago. Offbeat Ford products like the early Lincoln Cosmopolitan, the 1950-51 Ford Crestline, plastic-top Mercury Sun Valley and Ford Victoria are rising in price, but not as rapidly. The four-seat (post-1957) Thunderbirds have caught on, with a club of their own like their two-seat predecessors.

But Ford, Lincoln and Mercury still offer a lot of "sleepers." A very small group of knowledgeable enthusiasts has been quietly laying away "road race" 1952-54 Lincolns, for example. Though they were the dominant American cars in the 1952-54 Mexican Road Race, they have been largely overlooked, and prices are attractive. These Lincolns were among the most cleanly styled, best-built, finest-performing models of the period. They're well worth considering.

While 1955-57 Chevrolets have a following of maybe 8000 collectors, Fords of the same period have attracted only a 10th of that number. It's hard to understand why. The 1955-57 Fords were built in similar quantities. They were good cars with many interesting features: a lively overhead-valve V8 engine, genuine safety engineering, sleek styling and colorful interiors. Selling for as little as $1500 in good condition (perhaps half the price of an equivalent Chevy), they offer interesting second-car transportation. But it probably will be many more years before they increase greatly in value.

When it comes to Thunderbirds, two-seaters have a long lead. They were among the first models to benefit from concentrated attention: as used cars, their prices hit bottom and started going up again very soon after production ended. Today, the two clubs for them number over 6000 members. Four-seaters from 1958 on are priced at thousands of dollars less. Their styling is not as pure and simple as that of the two-seaters, but they're good investments and satisfying highway cars.

Except for Thunderbirds, the postwar Ford movement seems to have skipped over the 1950s. Edsels may be the exception, because people are fascinated by them as multimillion-dollar mistakes—out-of-production orphans. But comparable Fords, Mercurys and Lincolns are not yet collected in really large numbers. Today the big new interest is in the Mustangs of the early '60s. This leaves collectors of the earlier Ford Lincoln or Mercury models in an advantageous position.

The Edsel, needless to say, is controversial. Two large clubs have created a demand for it, but supply has thus far kept up with that demand. Whether you regard it as a technological masterpiece or the single most decadent car of the '50s will largely govern your consideration of one for your garage. But prices, except for Citation convertibles, are not imposing.

General Motors. Corvettes of all vintages are the most desirable postwar GM cars today, and Corvettes of the '50s are probably the most desirable of the entire group. The price spiral was late in coming, but when it arrived it hit hard. Today, one of the rare 1953 or 1955 'Vettes can cost up to $25,000. And that's not just an asking price; such amounts are actually being paid.

For those who think that Corvettes are all chrome and plastic and are overrated, there are plenty of other GM choices. The leading one of the 1950s seems to be the 1955-57 Chevrolet. These cars offered clean styling on modestly sized bodies, and some of the finest V8 engines ever designed. The vast quantity of them (five million for the three years) means that demand has not yet outstripped supply. So the '55-57 Chevy is one of the few really hotly desired collector cars you can still buy for a decent price. Nomads, convertibles and other Bel Air models are the most desirable, especially when equipped with V8s.

There is a smaller but growing interest in Pontiacs, Buicks and Oldsmobiles of the 1950s, all being served by strong clubs. Naturally, demand varies directly with rarity. Low-production specials like the 1953 Olds Fiesta and 1953-54 Buick Skylark are widely sought after. So are Pontiac's limited-production Bonnevilles and Safari station wagons (the ones based on Nomad, 1955-57). To some degree, Buicks and Pontiacs of the '50s are overshadowed by their counterparts from the '60s, the Riviera and the early GTO. This leaves the collector in a position to buy a 1950s model without mortgaging his house. With these exceptions, there is little interest in the 1958-59 Buick-Olds-Pontiac cars, though this may change.

Cadillac is the most generally collectible postwar GM make. Every year, every model is a good one. If the car is clean and original, so much the better. The 1953 and subsequent Eldorados are in great demand; their prices forbidding. (Conversely, strong collector interest has raised the price of 1948 and 1949 models, so the 1950-53 cars are more affordable than those earlier ones.)

Kaiser-Frazer, Willys. Traditionally the least costly collectibles of the 1950s, this group has shown very stable prices over the years of hobby expansion. This probably results from relatively low demand. The K-F club, covering only nine model years, has never topped 1800 members. One exception is the Darrin sports car, of which only 435 were built. Even though about three-fourths of these are known, the demand is huge. Prices as high as $15,000 have been asked, and at least $10,000 has been paid.

Lower K-F price scales make for many interesting buys. The most collectible Frazer of the 1950s is no doubt the '51, the last of the line. Obviously, the four-door hardtop and convertible Manhattans (like their 1950 Kaiser counterparts) are strongly priced. Sedan and Vagabond prices run much lower, and these cars offer some bonuses. Vagabonds double as high-cargo utility cars; 1951 Frazer standard sedans have the deluxe interior that was also used in the 1950 Frazer Manhattan.

Dutch Darrin's 1951-53 Kaiser may have been the purest full-size sedan designed in the 1950s. Prices rarely range beyond $2000, except for the limited-production Dragons. But even Dragons are affordable compared to special editions from other manufacturers. A Dragon may sell for a third of the price of a Packard Caribbean in comparable condition.

Relatively high interest surrounds the 1954-55 Kaisers with their beautiful styling and aircraft-like interior. Manhattans, with the McCulloch supercharger, are preferred to unblown Specials. Prices are not bad, though, and parts and expertise are available. Though the Kaiser Six was never designed for varying rpm in automotive applications, it was originally an industrial engine, K-F buffs and modern technology can keep troubles to a minimum. In good condition, it is a lively yet very economical power plant.

Small attention has been paid to the Henry J, while the Allstate's rarity makes it highly desirable. The Willys Aeros have a small but devoted following. Jeepsters have more, and are the focus of two specialist clubs. Willys cars of the '50s deserve more attention than they get.

Studebaker-Packard. Beyond any question, the Studebaker "Loewy coupes" of 1953-54 are the best buys today among all cars of the '50s. Their styling was so timeless and so good that they were cited as a landmark design when they were new.

There's no mystery behind the coupe's low price: there are a lot of them left. Studebaker enthusiasts tend to think first of Hawks and Avantis. Coupes were not blessed with the same kind of performance or the deluxe interiors of those later models. Right now, you can still find a nice Starliner hardtop or Starlight coupe in Commander V8 or Champion Six form for less than $2000. There are plenty to go around.

Generally speaking, postwar Studebakers are not too expensive. The most interesting from the early years are the Starlight coupes with wraparound rear window. Naturally, 1950-51 convertibles are rare and more expensive. For 1955, the greatest interest surrounds the luxurious President Speedster, with its deluxe interior and turned metal dash.

Studebaker Hawks of 1956 onward are high-demand items, though there are differences between them. Most expensive are the 1956-58 Golden Hawks. The 1956 Flight-Power-Sky Hawks and 1957-59 Silver Hawks remain good buys and are more efficient for use as second cars. Flight Hawks are six-cylinder cars; the rest are V8s. The V8s are not supercharged, though, and are easier on gas.

Other unique but not high-priced Studebakers with some demand among collectors are the 1952 and 1958 Starlight hardtops (only one model year for each of those bodies), and the 1959 Lark hardtops.

Literally every Packard is a blue-chip collector's item, and has been for a long time. Clippers (1956) and Packard Clippers (1953-55) are commensurately cheaper; but even so, a good one will set you back a fair amount of money. There are interesting distinctions between certain models, however, that do allow some Packards to sell for less than others which are similar.

In the 1951-54 period, a Mayfair hardtop (1951-53) is less costly than a Pacific hardtop (1954), because the latter was slightly more luxurious and is very rare. If you can't afford a Caribbean, consider the 250 convertible, which was the same car with less radical trim. Among Caribbeans themselves, the 1953-54 models seem better buys to us than the 1955-56 models, which tend now to sell for more. We think the earlier models will ultimately be worth more. But no Caribbean is cheap; prices are well over $5000 for anything capable of *concours* competition.

Among Clippers, the Super hardtop will run less than the Constellation, just as it did when new. Likewise, the Constellation is priced below the Packard Executive, which in turn is less than the Packard Four Hundred, in turn less than the '56 Caribbean hardtop. Prices here tend to align with the original model hierarchy.

PHOTO CREDITS: American Motors Corp.; Chrysler Corp.; Cunningham Automotive Museum; Dragonwyck Publishing Ltd.; Ford Archives; Ford Motor Co.; Henry Ford Museum; General Motors—Buick Division, Cadillac Division, Chevrolet Division, Oldsmobile Division, Pontiac Division; A. Hall; Bud Juneau; Duncan MacRae; National Automotive History Collection, Detroit Public Library; Neil Perry; R. Perry Zavitz.

Allstate

**Sears, Roebuck & Co.,
Via Kaiser-Frazer Corp., Willow Run, Michigan**

It's hard to imagine a blue-chip company like Sears, Roebuck making a mistake as big as the Henry J-based Allstate, but it did. Sears' Allstate Insurance bought one for posterity in 1971, and that was the company's first admission since about 1955 that the car was real. Until then, personnel at Sears auto parts counters had denied it ever existed.

The Allstate had seemed like a good idea. Theodore V. Houser, Sears' vice-president for merchandising, wanted a complete car to sell, along with parts and accessories, at his new chain of auto shops adjacent to Sears retail outlets. A Kaiser-Frazer hookup was a natural. At the time, Houser was buying Homart enamelware from Kaiser Metals (in which Sears held a 45 percent share) and had been a member of the K-F board since 1949. Edgar Kaiser, K-F's president, somehow convinced his dealers to accept a department store as a competitor, and the Allstate was announced in November 1951. It was the only new make for 1952, and the first car offered by Sears since the highwheeler of 1912.

Based strictly on the Henry J, the Allstate featured a new face by designer Alex Tremulis, special identification and a major interior upgrading. Sears followed its practice of improving on proprietary products. K-F's interior specialist, Carleton Spencer, used quilted saran plastic combined with a coated paper fiber encapsulated in vinyl, a material he'd discovered in use on the transatlantic telegraph cable. It seemed absolutely impervious to normal wear. The cars wore Allstate tires and tubes, batteries and spark plugs: the tires were guaranteed for 18 months, the battery was guaranteed for 24 months, and the rest of the package was covered for 90 days or 4000 miles. Standard on all Allstates (but not all Henry Js) was an opening trunk deck and dashboard glove box. Sears aggressively offered five trim and engine versions against Henry J's four, and priced its basic four-cylinder Allstate at $1395, just under the price

1952 Allstate marketed by Sears, Roebuck. $1395-1693.

Proposed Allstate wagon by Brooks Stevens.

of the standard Henry J.

But the idea failed. Whether it failed because people didn't take to buying a car in a department store or because of a narrow marketing approach in the Southeast is difficult to determine. Only 1566 Allstates were built for '52, and only 797 for '53. Then Sears canceled the project. With it died plans for the future, including attractive two-door station wagons proposed by industrial designer Brooks Stevens and Gordon Tercey of Kaiser-Frazer.

Today, Allstates are extremely rare and are considered more desirable than Henry J models from those years. The Allstate's demise enabled most Kaiser-Frazer dealers to breathe a sigh of relief—but not quite as big a sigh as Sears heaved.

ALLSTATE AT A GLANCE 1950-1959

Model Year	1950	1951	1952	1953	1954	1955	1956	1957	1958	1959
Price Range, $			1395-1693	1528-1785						
Weight Range, Lbs.			2300-2355	2405-2455						
Wheelbases, Ins.			100	100						
4 Cyl Engines, BHP			68	68						
6 Cyl Engines, BHP			80	80						

Buick

**Buick Motor Division of General Motors Corp.,
Flint, Michigan**

Three different styling periods, a 50th anniversary, and the advent of V8 engines marked Buick history in the '50s. Throughout the decade, Buicks were big, powerful, sometimes garish cars that reflected what could be considered either the best contemporary thinking or the worst depravity of those glittery years before the advent of Big Three compacts, pollution controls and safety regulations. The Buicks of the 1950s are very different cars from the Buicks of today; yet the two generations share a tradition of quality, high performance in their class, and product lines carefully orchestrated to fit the times and the market.

The 1949 restyling that affected all General Motors lines resulted in the lowest, sleekest Buicks in history, but there was more to come in 1950. If '49 had been the Year of the Porthole, '50 was the Year of the Sweep-spear; both items remained Buick trademarks through the '50s and beyond. For the 1950-53 period, the lineup included Specials, Supers and Roadmasters. Specials were sleekly styled and rode on a 121.5-inch wheelbase. They were competitively priced cars designed to catch third-place Plymouth in the production race. The Special began as a series of utilitarian standard and deluxe models in four-door and two-door sedans, a sedanet (coupe) and a business coupe. Later, attractive, sporty hardtops and convertibles were added to the series. Buick's pioneering two-door Riviera hardtop of 1949 continued in the Super and Roadmaster lines and extended to the Special by 1951. The Riviera name was also applied to a very well-proportioned four-door sedan in the Super and Roadmaster series, which used its own extended wheelbase (125.5 for the Super; 130.25 for the

Roadmaster). There also were two woody wagons, which Buick would offer through 1953. These cars—with wooden body parts made of mahogany and white ash—were big, expensive haulers: the 1953 Roadmaster estate wagon cost $4031 and weighed 4315 pounds. They had their own special wheelbase in the Roadmaster series.

From 1950 to 1952, and in the 1953 Special, Buick continued to rely on its aging but proven valve-in-head straight Eight. Its displacement, compression and horsepower varied model to model. The base Special engine of 1950 displaced 248.1 cubic inches and produced 115 horsepower, or 120 horsepower with Dynaflow automatic drive, a Special option through the end of the series in 1958. Supers and 1951-53 Specials used the 263 cubic-inch engine offering horsepower as high as 130; Roadmasters used a hefty 320 cubic-inch unit, which by 1952 was developing 170 bhp at 3800 rpm.

Dynaflow Drive—some called it Dyna-slush—had been introduced on the Roadmaster in late 1947. Standard on Roadmasters, it became an increasingly popular option on other models at around $200. This torque converter system depended on induced rotation of a drive turbine by a crankshaft-driven facing turbine through an oil bath. Dynaflow was smooth, but not too exciting in terms of performance. The Twin Turbine Dynaflow of 1953 was a more positive two-speed version; and by the end of the decade, an even better Triple Turbine setup was offered across the board as a $296 option. But Dynaflow in all its forms lacked the accelerative abilities of Hydra-matic, and was therefore handicapped in an age of horsepower and hot rods.

1950 Special sedanet, $1856.

1951 Super convertible, priced at $2728.

Buick

Golden Anniversary year 1953 was significant for power steering, 12-volt electrics, and Buick's fine new overhead-valve V8 in the Super and Roadmaster. The V8 was an oversquare (4x3.25-inch bore and stroke) unit of 322 cubic inches that developed up to 188 hp at 4000 rpm, thanks to an industry-topping 8.5:1 compression ratio.

That year also saw the debut of the limited-edition Skylark sports convertible, a car for flashy Hollywood types and Texas oil men. Buick made only 1690 of them, and priced them at an extraordinary $5000. Many custom features were standard.

Skylark was another of those Harley Earl styling projects for which GM had long been famous; yet, typical of GM's way of thinking, it was designed for the broadest possible appeal. Instead of being a two-seat sports car—those accounted for only 0.27 percent of the market in 1953—it was a luxurious, sporty personal car of the same type as Ford's

1952 Roadmaster Riviera hardtop, $3306.

1953 Skylark sport convertible, $5000.

1953 Roadmaster Riviera sedan with air, $3700.

Thunderbird and Buick's own Rivieras of the '60s. Like the similar Oldsmobile Fiesta and Cadillac Eldorado, the Skylark was a large convertible, chopped and sectioned: four inches were removed from the windshield height; the top was correspondingly lower. Skylark was much cleaner looking than standard Buicks. It had no portholes and no hubcaps, but sported the Kelsey Hayes chrome wire wheels that were coming into fashion throughout the industry by 1953.

Skylark was back again the following year, but the '54 was a much less radical car that sold for only $4483. It arrived with tack-on tailfins and huge, chrome-plated, die-cast taillight housings. Its open-wheel design approximated that of the Wildcat II show car. Apparently, the 1954 version impressed people less than the '53 had, for only 836 were sold and the series was discontinued for 1955.

Buick's show cars of the '50s were among the wildest in the industry. Led by the XP-300 and LeSabre of 1951, they were rolling laboratories—test vehicles for a number of unique ideas.

Both the XP-300 and the LeSabre used an experimental 215 cubic-inch aluminum V8. It was not a forebear of the 215 V8 of the '60s, but a very special job, exactly square with a 3.25x3.25-inch bore and stroke. It boasted a 10:1 compression ratio and over 300 horsepower. Induction was boosted by a Roots-type supercharger; the fuel it used was a combination of methanol and gasoline.

Styling of the two cars, which had wheelbases of 115 to 116 inches, was radical: LeSabre sported the wraparound windshield and the Dagmar bumpers that would come into prominence a few years later; the XP-300 used the concave grille and mesh-backed headlamp nacelles that would be seen on the production '54s.

Buick production had meanwhile ground on inexorably toward the industry's number three spot. The company broke an all-time record in 1950 by assembling more than 550,000 cars. When Flint built 531,000 units in 1954, Buick found itself behind only Chevrolet and Ford—a position it had not held since 1930. In 1955, Buick built 781,000 cars, not only a new record but nearly a 50 percent increase over its highest previous figure. This success was based largely on the strength of the Special, which had grown to become one of the industry's best sellers.

Sales of the Special began moving when the model gained a 264 V8 cubic-inch in 1954, but in banner year 1955 it was everywhere: over 380,000 were made, including 155,000 Riviera two-door hardtops, the most popular single model of the day. The entire Buick line had been restyled in 1954, with a longer, squarer body style and wraparound windshield.

Buicks became really fast cars. The Century series of 1954 used a 195-horsepower V8 and a smaller, lighter Special body. It immediately became the "hot" Buick.

Four-door and two-door Rivieras in the Special and Century series arrived in 1955, and were joined by Super and Roadmaster versions in 1956. The rest of the industry scampered to catch up while Buick dealers enjoyed unprecedented success.

The mild face lift for 1956 produced a similar range of cars that didn't sell as well in that anticlimactic year. The division began affixing dates to the cars' exteriors, but this practice was abandoned as soon as buyers began to notice that they were proclaiming ownership of last year's model. With the horsepower race in full swing, the '56s were more powerful than Buicks had ever been. The Specials delivered 220 hp and the rest of the line provided 255. A '56 Buick Century could leap from 0 to 60 mph in 10½ seconds and exceed 110 mph, and there wasn't a Buick in the line that couldn't exceed 100 mph.

The line was fully restyled again in '57. Ed Ragsdale, Buick's general manager, never said how much the 1957 restyling had cost, but it must have cost several hundred million. Despite the most sweeping alterations since 1949, the cars didn't sell particularly well, possibly because their rivals were pressing hard. At Chrysler, Virgil Exner's tailfinned "Forward Look" had been introduced, Highland Park was selling almost as many cars as it had sold in 1955, and Plymouth was forging its way back into third place. But the '57 Buicks were clean, well-styled cars. Model additions were few but significant: a new four-door hardtop station wagon in the Special series; and a new Series 75 Roadmaster

1951 XP-300 with designer-engineer Chayne.

1951 Le Sabre, a real show-stopper.

1954 Century DeLuxe sedan, priced at $2520.

1955 Century convertible, priced at $2991.

1956 Roadmaster Riviera hardtop sedan, $3692.

1957 Century Riviera hardtop, $3270.

Buick

1958 Special two-door sedan, $2836.

1959 Electra 225 convertible, $4867.

hastily contrived, chrome-bespangled tailfins, the Limited was hideous. So were the other '58 Buicks. They didn't sell, but their awful styling was not the biggest reason for their decline. The 1958 recession is what hurt them most. Buick production dropped to 250,000 cars, and the division slipped behind Oldsmobile to fifth place. These '58 Buicks were the fattest ones since the war: they were some 400 pounds heavier than the 1950 models and three to four inches longer than the '57s. Air suspension was offered, but was not ordered by many. Altogether, it was a very bad year.

So was 1959. If the '58s had been gross, the '59s went the other way in a peak year for Buick styling. Though dominated by the now-omnipresent tailfin, the '59 was at least smooth, clean and fairly dignified (there were fewer chrome squares, too). Their A bodies were now shared with other GM lines, but it wasn't obvious. Gone were the traditional model names: the Special was renamed LeSabre, the Century became Invicta, the Super and Roadmaster were dubbed Electra and Electra 225. At the bottom end, LeSabre and Invicta retained the old Special/Century body styles. The hardtop wagon, which hadn't sold well, was dropped. The two Electras were priced between $3810 and $4300, down quite a bit from 1958, and they rode slightly shorter wheelbases. They were called 1959's most changed cars, and the change was for the better.

There were some new mechanical developments for 1959: a 401 cubic-inch V8 of 325 horsepower (4.2x3.6 bore and stroke) was built for the upper three models, the 364 V8 was used in the LeSabre. Power brakes and steering were standard on Electras, a $150 option for the other series. Air conditioning was a $430 extra. Air suspension, which was available for only the rear wheels, was not popular.

Significantly, Buick dealers were selling more Opels in 1959 than ever before. The German captive import assigned to Buick in 1958 grabbed an increasing number of customers as people saw penalties in oversize, overweight automobiles. But Buick Division was already planning its own compact, the 1961 Skylark, and its star would rise again. The division would sell over 700,000 cars in 1969.

that was basically a series 70, offering every possible accessory except air conditioning as standard. Series 75s came with Dynaflow, power steering, power brakes, flexspoke steering wheels, dual exhausts, automatic windshield washers and wide-angle wipers, backup lights, clocks, special interiors with deep-pile carpeting and a host of minor features. Though a good year for Buick, '57 was an even better year for Plymouth, which knocked Buick out of third place.

In those days, the answer to sales problems seemed to be more chrome, and thus arrived the 1958s, the ugliest Buicks in history. There's a young stylist in Detroit who drives an enormous pink 1958 Buick Limited in a quiet rebellion against today's crisp styles. He couldn't have picked a better car. From a monstrous grille that contains 160 chrome squares within a huge shell to its

BUICK AT A GLANCE 1950-1959

Model Year	1950	1951	1952	1953	1954	1955	1956	1957	1958	1959
Price Range, $	1803-3433	2046-3780	2115-3977	2197-5000	2207-4483	2233-3552	2357-3704	2596-4483	2636-5125	2740-4300
Weight Range, Lbs.	3615-4470	3600-4470	3620-4505	3675-4315	3690-4355	3715-4415	3750-4395	3955-4539	4058-4710	4159-4660
Wheelbases, Ins.	121.5-130.25	121.5-130.25	121.5-130.25	121.5-125.5	122-127	122-127	122-127	122-127.5	122-127.5	123-126.25
8 Cyl Engines, BHP	115-152	120-152	120-170	125-188	143-200	188-236	220-255	250-300	250-300	250-325

Cadillac

Cadillac Division of General Motors Corp., Detroit, Michigan

Cadillacs of the early '50s were among the best road cars of their era. The 1950 series 61—relatively light and equipped with a 160-horsepower V8, standard shift and 3.77 rear axle ratio—was the fastest passenger car in the United States, according to enthusiast Ed Gaylord of Chicago.

"I owned one of these and a new Jaguar XK-120 at the time," Gaylord said, "and the Cadillac was the faster car up to about 90 mph. My Cadillac set what was then a stock car record at the original quarter-mile drag races in Santa Ana, California . . . The only competition I had in acceleration was from the small 135-horsepower Olds 88 coupe, but the Cadillac engine was substantially more efficient both in performance and economy."

If drag racing isn't proof positive, consider the international racing results: Briggs Cunningham campaigned a near-stock Coupe de Ville and a Cadillac with a special body at Le Mans in 1950, finishing 10th and 11th overall—and the stock car came in ahead of the special. Further up in the finishing column was an Allard J2 which ran third, powered by the same Cadillac V8 engine.

Cadillac's revolutionary tailfin styling made its debut in 1948. A short-stroke, overhead-valve V8 arrived in '49. This one-two punch put Cadillac firmly on top in the luxury-car field, and it is still there. Lincoln wasn't competing with a wide enough range of models; Packard had for years emphasized its medium-priced standard Eights; Chrysler's Imperial wasn't really in the same league as far as buyers in this class were concerned. Cadillac fielded a four-model lineup in 1950 that started at $2761 (although few were sold for less than $3000) and reached up to about $5000 for the long-wheelbase Fleetwood 75 sedans and limousines. In addition, the division provided most of the chassis for special body builders, averaging about 2000 per year from 1950 to 1959 for hearses, flower cars and other uses.

The Cadillac V8 was introduced with a displacement of 331 cubic inches and was not enlarged until 1956; but it gained over 100 horsepower in the intervening years, ending with 270 hp in the 1955 Eldorado. Designed by Ed Cole, John Gordon and Harry Barr, the V8 had begun to develop before the war, when Cadillac realized that its old L-head V8 was reaching the limit of compression and would not be able to take advantage of the high-octane fuels that were promised. (According to Harry Barr, the 331 had far more compression capability than was ever used. He said it could have gone as high as 12:1, but that sort of

1951 Sixty-two Coupe de Ville. Price: $3843.

1952 Sixty-two sedan, priced at $3684.

octane never became available.) The engine featured five main bearings, wedge-shaped combustion chambers, a slightly shorter stroke than bore ($3 \frac{13}{16}$ x $3\frac{5}{8}$), and slipper pistons with cutaway skirts for lightness and low reciprocating weight. The total weight saving was great: the 1950 V8 weighed about 200 pounds less than the 1948 L-head. Combined with GM Hydra-matic, which was standard on all '50s Cadillacs except the GI series, the cars were smooth and powerful machines—demonstrably superior in performance to rival heavyweights powered by less vigorous drive trains.

The most unfortunate thing about Cadillac in the '50s was its gradual trend away from clean styling and toward chrome-laden glitter. This trend reached a peak in 1958-59; a return to conservative architecture began in the 1960s. But Harley Earl's and Bill Mitchell's styling of the 1948 Cadillac had been so good that a lot of face-lifting was needed to alter it. According to Bill Mitchell, a traditional look was always preserved from year to year. "If a grille is changed," he said, "the tail end is left

Cadillac

alone; if a fin is changed, the grille is not monkeyed with." Through 1953, the changes were small: a one-piece windshield in 1950, small auxiliary grilles under the headlamps in 1951, a winged badge in that spot for 1952, Dagmar bumpers and a one-piece rear window in 1953.

Together with Oldsmobile and Buick in 1949, Cadillac had pioneered the two-door hardtop convertible. The Caddy was the more successful of the three, since Coupe de Ville production was always a higher percentage for Cadillac than Riviera was for Buick or Holiday was for Olds.

The model lineup did not change much in the first design period of 1950-53, either. The 62 series, accounting for most sales, comprised a four-door sedan, coupe, Coupe de Ville and convertible; the 60 Special was a sedan with a wheelbase of 130 inches instead of 126; the 75 series limousine and sedan rode a wheelbase of 146.75 inches. The 61 was the postwar successor to the LaSalle, available in sedan or coupe form on a shorter 122-inch wheelbase. Manual shift was standard, and the 61 sold for some $575 less than the 62. But by 1952, Cadillac had dropped the 61. Cadillac's traditional archrival Packard, in contrast, pushed cars that sold for as much as $750 less than the cheapest Cadillac in 1951, abandoning its original field almost completely. That was a mistake—one that Packard realized too late.

Limited editions from GM in 1953 included the Cadillac Eldorado. Only 532 were built. They were priced at $7750, a figure that made the Eldorado the most expensive car of that year by far. Like Buick's Skylark, the Eldorado featured a custom interior and special cut-down panoramic windshield. A metal boot covered the lowered convertible top. It was indeed a striking car. Cadillacs could be purchased with Dynaflow automatic transmissions in '53, because a fire in the Hydramatic plant at Willow Run forced Cadillac to use some Buick units.

Model year 1954 was a year of restyling at GM. It brought longer, lower, wider and more powerful Cadillacs. Wheelbases were lengthened: up to 129 inches for the 62s; 133 for the 60 Specials. The 75s retained their old chassis. The 331 engine got a boost in horsepower to 230. Cadillac reduced the price of the Eldorado to $5738, and as a result, 2150 were sold. Sales doubled for 1955. For '56, the line expanded to include a Seville coupe and Biarritz convertible, each priced at $6556. From 1955 onward, Eldorados were distinctively styled with sharply pointed fins over round taillights; the rest

1953 Sixty-two convertible, $4144.

1953 Eldorado convertible, $7750.

1954 Sixty-two convertible, $4404.

1955 Sixty-two sedan, priced at $3977.

of the line continued to use the small taillight and fin design that had become a Cadillac trademark. Division sales, which had topped 100,000 units for the first time in 1950, continued to improve through the middle years of the decade. In 1955, Cadillac sold 153,334 units, the highest number ever. Even this was a temporary plateau, for production would break 200,000 in the '60s and reach 266,000 by 1969. Despite momentary challenges by a revitalized Imperial in 1957 and a crisp Lincoln Continental in 1961, Cadillac was never really threatened. Neither Lincoln nor Imperial ever built more than 40,000 cars in a year. In the 1950s, more than at any other time in its history, Cadillac was unchallenged as Standard of the World.

The line was restyled again for 1957, inspired by the Eldorado Brougham and Park Avenue show cars. The new $13,000 Eldorado Brougham of '57 was one of Cadillac's most interesting cars. It took its inspiration from the Orleans, Park Avenue and Brougham show cars of 1953-55. The Eldo Brougham was a pillarless sedan with doors that opened in the center and a brushed aluminum roof, which was one of Harley Earl's favorite styling ideas. Its quadruple headlights were a first for the industry—shared with Nash—that predicted headlight design from 1959 onward.

The Eldo also was equipped with air suspension, which had been in use since 1952, but not on a passenger car. The Eldorado Brougham's air suspension was designed by engineers Lester Milliken and Fred Cowin, two longtime Cadillac staffers. It used an air spring at each wheel that was made up of a dome air chamber, rubber diaphragm and pistons. The domes were fed by a central air compressor and were continually adjusted for load and road conditions by valves and solenoids. It kept the Brougham level and smoothed its ride. The Cadillac system differed from that offered as an option by other GM divisions because it was an open system that took air from the outside atmosphere; the other system was closed, with a pressure tank and associated plumbing.

But the cost and complexity of the air suspension proved too high in comparison to its benefits. The air domes leaked, dealer replacements were frequent, and many Broughams that had had air suspension required replacement coil springs in later years. The system was dropped four years after its introduction.

The Brougham itself, after only two years of production during which a total of 704 cars were built, was completely restyled in Detroit and was farmed out to Pininfarina of Italy. Only 99 were assembled in 1959; 101 were built in 1960.

The 1958 Cadillacs, as well as cars from the other GM divisions, were among the most garish ever built. They were big, heavy cars laden with bright-

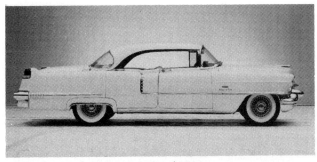
1956 Sixty-two Sedan de Ville, $4753.

1957 Sixty-two Coupe de Ville, $5116.

1958 Eldorado Brougham, $13,074.

1959 De Ville hardtop. Price: $5252.

Cadillac

1958 Eldorado Biarritz convertible, $7500.

1958 Sixty Special, priced at $6232.

1959 Sixty Special, priced at $6233.

been since 1954. The De Ville had become a special series, pillared sedans had been temporarily eliminated, and the 62 series had been expanded to include a special four-door sedan model with an extended deck. The engine, which had been bored to 365 cubic inches for 1956, was developing 310 horsepower by 1958. All Cadillacs were available with cruise control, high pressure cooling, two-speaker radio with automatic signal-seeking tuner, and automatic-release parking brakes. There was even a special show Eldorado with a "thinking" convertible top that raised itself and the side windows when it sensed rain.

An important year for Cadillac was 1959. The restyling resulted in tailfins that expanded ridiculously, but the cars got a new 390 cubic-inch engine of 325 to 345 horsepower, some suspension improvements and better power steering. The line-up included four- and six-window sedans. This was the last year for the old 75 chassis, which was finally updated in 1960. The cars were generally more expensive than before, with 62s selling for around $5000 and Eldorados going for $7400 and up. But Cadillac built 138,000 units for the calendar year and was satisfied with its performance.

Also featured for 1959 was a show car called the Cadillac Cyclone, a custom with a 104-inch wheelbase, four-wheel independent suspension, integral frame construction and a clear plastic canopy top that was coated inside with vaporized silver to reflect the sun's rays. The canopy slid away as the door was opened. At the touch of a button, the passenger could slide the door back along the side of the car for easy entrance. Strictly an idea car, the Cyclone was a departing gift from Harley Earl, who had retired, being relieved as chief of design by Bill Mitchell. Under Mitchell, Cadillacs would take on a more dignified posture and subdued tailfins for the '60s.

But it had been a great 10 years—the greatest, in terms of expansion, in Cadillac's history. Starting with a car designed for the very wealthy in 1950, Cadillac became the standard for young individuals on the way up as well. With average American income rising faster than Cadillac's prices, more people were driving the Standard of the World than ever before.

work. They were less memorable by far than the 1953 Eldorado or the 1957-58 Eldorado Brougham. Sales were poor in that recession year: Cadillac production, at 125,501 units, was lower than it had

CADILLAC AT A GLANCE 1950-1959

Model Year	1950	1951	1952	1953	1954	1955	1956	1957	1958	1959
Price Range, $	2761-4959	2831-5405	3587-5643	3571-7750	3838-6090	3882-6402	4201-6828	4677-13,074	4784-13,074	4892-13,075
Weight Range, Lbs.	3822-4586	3807-4652	4140-4733	4225-4850	4365-4815	4358-5113	4420-5130	4565-5390	4630-5425	4690-5490
Wheelbases, Ins.	122-146.75	122-146.75	126-146.75	126-147	129-149.75	129-149.75	129-149.75	129-149.75	129.5-149.75	130-149.75
8 Cyl Engines, BHP	160	160	190	210	230	250-270	285-305	300-325	310-325	325-345

Chevrolet

Chevrolet Division of General Motors Corp., Detroit, Michigan

In the decade of the 1950s, the Chevrolet evolved from a staid family car to a hot performance car; the division moved from building dull sedans to building dull sedans and fast sports cars. Chevy also dropped from number one in the industry to number two—but only briefly.

Most of Chevy's decisions between 1950 and 1959 were the right ones. It was right to build the Corvette, even though only 674 were sold in the car's third year of production. It was right to build the Bel Air, first as a hardtop and later as an individual series, because by 1957 Bel Airs were dominating production with over 700,000 units. It was right to build the 265 and 283 cubic-inch V8s, in that they changed Chevrolet's image almost overnight. And it was right to produce the Impala, because it upgraded the character of the top of the line, causing Chevrolets to be considered by people who previously would have bought Pontiacs or—worse yet—Dodges and Mercurys.

The early years of 1950-52 were the last of the traditional low-cost, low-suds Chevys: 1953-54 saw a transition; 1955 a revolution. In the early period there was the Special, which accounted for about 15 to 20 percent of the total production; and the DeLuxe, which accounted for the remainder and offered a wide variety of models. Specials came in four- or two-door sedans, in coupes and business coupes known as Styleline models, and in four- and two-door fastback sedans called Fleetlines. The Deluxe lineup had no business coupe, but comprised a wagon, hardtop, convertible and the Fleetline fastbacks.

Fleetlines sold well enough during the seller's market of 1946-50, but the fad had faded by the early '50s. Chevrolet quickly phased them out. The last was a two-door sedan in the 1952 Deluxe series, and only 37,000 were made. As rapidly as the fastbacks disappeared, Bel Air hardtops took their place. Chevrolet was a year ahead of Ford and Plymouth in introducing a pillarless coupe, and sales were brisk: 76,000 were sold in 1950; 103,000 were sold the following year. All 1950-52 Chevrolets were powered by the hoary old "stove bolt Six." This 216.5 cubic-inch mill with 3.5x3.75-inch bore and stroke delivered 92 horsepower at 3400 rpm, or 105 at 3600 when fitted with optional Powerglide two-speed automatic. Prices of Chevys in those years were competitive and styling was consistent, varying from '50 to '52 only in minor details like grille, taillights and side moldings.

In 1953, all GM cars got a major face lift, but Chevy and Pontiac looked newest. Chevy renamed the Special the One-Fifty and the Deluxe the

1950 DeLuxe Styleline four-door sedan, $1529.

1951 DeLuxe Styleline Bel Air hardtop, $1914.

1952 DeLuxe Styleline sport coupe, $1726.

Two-Ten; brought out the Bel Air as a series in its own right; and introduced America's first postwar sports car. The Corvette, a fiberglass two-seater selling for about $3500, almost disappeared early in its existence. Sporting motorists found it hard to reconcile themselves to its automatic transmission, even though its modified Six put out 150 horsepower. A V8 option made available by 1955 helped save the car, and Corvette went on to be-

Chevrolet

come one of GM's success stories.

The new Chevy Six of 1953 was an improved engine with much higher compression, a displacement of 235.5 cubic inches and up to 115 horsepower. It remained in use through the '50s and beyond, grinding out as much as 145 bhp in passenger cars. It was a sound and reliable engine, but not a very exciting one. Ed Cole's V8 took care of the excitement.

Without question, the 1955 V8, which had a displacement of 265 cubic inches, was one of the world's milestone engines. Though designed to be efficient and cheap to build, it was really one of those "blue sky" projects of the type that comes along only once or twice in an engineer's career. Said Ed Cole, "I had worked on V8 engines all my professional life. I had lived and breathed engines. [Motor engineer Harry F.] Barr and I were always saying how we would do it if we could ever design a new engine. You just know you want five main bearings—there's no decision to make. We knew that a certain bore-stroke relationship was the most compact. We knew we'd like a displacement of 265 cubic inches. . . And we never changed any of this.

Prototype sketches of first Corvette, 1953.

1956 Bel Air sport sedan V8, $2329.

1954 Bel Air sedan. Price: $1884.

1956 Corvette, probably a show car. Note narrow whites.

1955 Two-Ten hardtop, priced from $1959 to $2058.

1957 Bel Air Nomad station wagon V8, $2857.

We released our engine for tooling direct from the drawing boards—that's how crazy and confident we were."

Cole and Barr had reason to be enthusiastic. The 265 weighed even less than the Chevy Six. It had a low reciprocating weight which allowed high rpm; die-cast heads with integral, interchangeable valve guides; a 3.75x3-inch bore and stroke; aluminum slipper pistons; and a crankshaft of forged pressed steel instead of alloy iron. It performed beautifully, putting out 162 hp at 4400 rpm, or 180 hp at 4600 with Power-pak—a four-barrel carburetor and dual exhausts. It became the basis of all the great Chevy engines of the immediate future: the 225-horsepower '56 Corvette; and the bored-out 283 V8 of 1957 that was the first mass-production engine to offer one horsepower per cubic inch with fuel injection. Chevrolet developed a new 348 cubic-inch V8 as a big-car option for 1958, and it was a good one. But the 283 remained the best-known, best-loved engine of the period, earning the cars a reputation for performance that they had never had with Sixes.

Powerglide automatic, a torque converter using the Dynaflow principle, was an increasingly popular option in these years at a price under $200. Smooth in operation, it was well suited to all but the performance models. The performance cars were available with a manual or stick overdrive, three-speed Turboglide automatic from 1957 on, and an all-synchromesh four-speed manual from 1959 onward.

Styling was as much a part of the mid-1950s picture as was engineering. Harley Earl's Chevy design team—Clare MacKichan, Chuck Stebbins, Bob Veryzer, Carl Renner and others—worked under Harley's guideline: "Go all the way, then back off." Though the '55 didn't reach production looking the way it had in fanciful renderings, it wasn't far off. The beltline dip and wraparound windshield had been inspired by the Eldorado, Fiesta and Skylark limited editions of 1953; the egg-crate grille had been inspired by Ferrari, and was a favorite of Harley Earl. That grille was unpopular with the public though, so the 1956 version was broader and more conventional.

Carl Renner was the man responsible for the unique hardtop wagon called the Bel Air Nomad. Actually, the car was too impractical to be a wagon, too bulky to be a hardtop. It was, however, the ideal stylistic blending of both concepts. If it didn't sell well, it was more because two-door wagons were not popular than because of any styling disadvantages. The Nomad was relatively expensive, but truly the world has never seen as beautiful a station wagon. Had anybody else built it, the Nomad probably would be quite rare today; but its volume was high: 8530 were built in 1955; 8103 in 1956; 6534 in 1957.

One mild face lift of the line came about in '56, followed by another in '57. Both Ford and Plymouth were restyled in 1957, so Chevrolet suffered in comparisons of newness. Chevy had achieved record market penetration of close to 28 percent in 1956. That dropped in 1957. Yet the '57 face lift was a good one, and the engines previously described made the cars go as well as they looked. A '57 Bel Air four-door hardtop with the 270-hp engine would streak from 0 to 60 in 9.9 seconds, do the quarter mile in 17.5 seconds, and run up to well over 110 miles per hour. One-Fiftys with injected V8s were lighter and even faster.

Appropriately equipped 1955-57 Chevys were, and are, formidable competitors on race tracks. Before the Automobile Manufacturers Association recommended an end to participation in organized racing in 1957, the Chevys did quite well on NASCAR and other circuits. At the 1957 Daytona Speed Weeks, they added straight-line performance achievements. In class 4 (213 to 259 cubic inches) Chevrolets won the first three places in the two-way flying mile; in Class 5 (259 to 305 cubic inches) they took 33 out of 37 places and the best car averaged 131.076 mph. Chevy also won the 1957 Pure Oil Manufacturers Trophy with 574 points, against only 309 for runner-up Ford.

When the 1958s came out, it was noticed that the division was deemphasizing competition. The cars were softer, and most reviewers were disgusted.

1957 Bel Air Sport sedan, V8. Price: $2464.

1958 Bel Air sport sedan V8, $2618.

Chevrolet

1959 Impala sport sedan V8, $2782.

Said Uncle Tom McCahill, "When an ad man can't write about his product's success at Pikes Peak, Daytona Beach or Darlington, or how fast it gets away from a traffic light, what's he got left? All he can do is tell about the hand-woven Indian rugs on the floor, the Da Vinci sculptured door handles, or the 'ten miles per gallon' it averaged under the featherfoot of a professional economy jockey."

McCahill was right. The 1958 Chevys were longer, lower, wider, heavier and slower. Chevrolet was reaching for a new market sector, the solid, substantial Pontiac types that it had never gone after before—with such cars as the Impala. People who bought Impalas, then as now, didn't care about performance or handling. They wanted bigness and comfort, and the Impala delivered.

Despite a rough year for the U.S. economy, the division managed to build over 1.2 million cars in 1958 of which 60,000 were Impalas. That was a decent showing for a series consisting only of a hardtop and convertible. The One-Fifty became the Delray, the Biscayne replaced the Two-Ten. The Bel Air remained, with Impala as one model in that series for '58 only. "Station Wagon" became a separate series with no fewer than five models: the two-door Yeoman; four-door Yeoman, Brookwood and Nomad; and nine-passenger Brookwood. The '58 Nomad wasn't the same car it had been in 1955-57, but was a conventional wagon. It remained so through 1961, its last year.

Chevrolet probably deserves credit for bucking the tailfin trend in 1958, but it made up for this in 1959 with an overdecorated gull-wing tail, and a deck, as Tom McCahill said, "big enough to land a Piper Cub." It could have been worse. Carl Renner said one 1959 proposal was for an upright, Edsel-like central grille. He called it one of the ugliest things he'd ever seen. As it turned out, the front end of the '59 was relatively mild, but the rear was a thing from another world. This was the year Ford beat Chevy, and the Chevrolet's rear was vastly altered for 1960.

In 1959, the Delray disappeared. The lineup included the Biscayne, the Bel Air, Impala, and Station Wagon. All rode a 119-inch wheelbase, the largest in postwar history. Chevy growth between 1957 and 1959 was amazing. Wheelbases were up four inches, length by nearly eleven inches, width by seven inches; and weight increased by 300 pounds. The '59s were the first of the overstuffed generation that we would live with for the next 15 years. Only now is GM weaning the public from these enormous vehicles. At the time, of course, they made sense. In order to compete, the low-priced three—Ford, Chevy and Plymouth—needed larger and larger dimensions, cars the size of Cadillacs and Lincolns that would sell at half the price. Chevy led; Ford and Plymouth followed suit.

The Corvette came of age in the later 1950s. To succeed the stubby and slow 1953-55 models, Harley Earl developed a beautifully sculptured design with concave side decoration and a busy grille. Engine performance improvements put the Corvette in the 130-mph class before the end of the decade—that was in "street stock" form. The Earl styling lasted quite awhile, until the Sting Ray made its debut in 1963. The 1956-62 'Vette was an aggressive, racy-looking sports car whose appearance nicely matched its performance.

Chevrolet has made mistakes since the '50s, but the division made no major blunders in that decade. Every program Chevy undertook back then proved wise.

CHEVROLET AT A GLANCE 1950-1959

Model Year	1950	1951	1952	1953	1954	1955	1956	1957	1958	1959
Price Range, $	1329-1994	1460-2191	1530-2297	1524-3513	1539-3523	1593-2934	1734-3149	1885-3465	2013-3631	2160-3875
Weight Range, Lbs.	3025-3460	3040-3470	3045-3475	2705-3495	2705-3540	2620-3385	2764-3516	2730-3566	2793-3839	2840-4020
Wheelbases, Ins.	115	115	115	102-115	102-115	102-115	102-115	102-115	102-117.5	102-119
6 Cyl Engines, BHP	92-105	92-105	92-105	108-150	115-150	123-155	140	140	145	135
8 Cyl Engines, BHP						162-195	162-225	162-283	185-280	185-315

Chrysler

Chrysler Division of Chrysler Corp., Detroit, Michigan

As the 1950s began, Chrysler was a high-volume line comprising no fewer than seven different series and 22 models. As the decade ended, Chrysler was an upper-medium-priced line of only four basic series and 15 models. The line shrank as the Imperial became a separate make in 1955 and the Windsor six-cylinder cars were dropped after 1954. In the process, styling and engineering improved. Beginning as dowdy cars powered by plodding L-head engines in 1950, Chryslers became vital performance cars with exciting styling by 1955. They eventually wore some of the best-looking tailfins of the age.

The tailfins, which arrived in grafted form in 1956, were designed-in from 1957. They were the work of Virgil M. Exner, who joined Chrysler after leaving Studebaker in 1949. Exner's tastes ran to classic cars—meaning bold, upright radiator grilles, open-wheel designs and rakish lines throughout. What he found at Chrysler were the engineering-oriented boxes of K.T. Keller, outgoing Chrysler president. They wouldn't knock your eyes out, it was said, but they wouldn't knock your hat off, either. The trouble with Keller's theory was that people didn't want practical compact cars in the 1950s—at least, not people who bought Chryslers. The division was having sales troubles, and before Exner was able to get any completely new designs into production, Chrysler sank from annual sales of 160,000 units to barely 100,000.

The year 1950 was the second one for the boxy cars that had emerged as Chrysler's first postwar restyling. The 1950 line included several models that were on their way out.

The six-cylinder, 116-horsepower Royals, which sold for less than $2200, were dropped after '50.

Prior to 1950, there had been a wide variety of Town & Countrys—sedans, convertibles and even the industry's first hardtops. But in 1950 the exotic, wood-decorated Town & Country series was down to one model—the Newport, a hardtop powered by the 135-hp straight Eight and equipped with four-wheel disc brakes. By 1950 the Town & Country had served its purpose, which was to glamorize an unglamorous range of automobiles by offering something vividly different. Only 700 of the hardtops were sold in '50 at their $4000 price, and then the hardtop too was dropped. The Town & Country name remained on Chrysler station wagons after that, and is with us still. The Saratoga, a peripheral seller, was dropped after 1952.

For a short time there were standard and luxury versions of the Windsor and New Yorker. But by the time the "Hundred Million Dollar Look" arrived in

1950 Town & Country Newport hardtop, $4028.

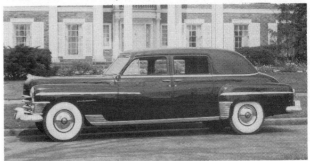
1950 Crown Imperial limousine, $5384

Hemi-powered '51 New Yorker pacing Indy 500.

1953 New Yorker De Luxe convertible, $3980.

Chrysler

Exner's first Ghia-bodied show car, the K-310.

1954 Imperial Newport, priced at $4560.

1955 New Yorker De Luxe sedan, $3494.

1956 New Yorker Newport four-door hardtop, $4102.

1955, the Chrysler lineup was down to just two models, sans Imperial, which had become a separate make in its own right.

It's easy to summarize the 1950-54 Chryslers because they were so much alike. All of them but the Crown Imperials and the long-wheelbase Windsor sedan were built on 125.5- or 131.5-inch wheelbases. (The Imperial rode on a 145.5-inch wheelbase; the long Windsor had a 139.5-inch wheelbase.) All were styled pretty much the same way.

The 1950-52 models were bolt-upright versions. The '50 models wore broad, chrome, egg-crate smiles; the 1951-52 models had a more conservative three-bar grille. There was no significant difference between the 1951 and the 1952 Chryslers, and the firm didn't even keep separate production figures for the two years. The only way to tell the cars apart at a glance is by the taillights, which had built-in back-up lamps in '52.

The Windsor (formerly the Royal) offered sedan, club coupe, wagon and long-wheelbase sedan; the Windsor De Luxe came in a wide variety of body styles including a long-wheelbase sedan and limousine, hardtop and convertible, and a special Traveler utility sedan in 1950 and 1951. Saratoga, while it lasted, offered a sedan and a club coupe, plus a wagon in 1951 and 1952 and a long sedan in '52 only. It was the quickest Chrysler, and a notable stock-car contender using a hemi V8 in the shorter Windsor wheelbase. New Yorkers came in roughly the same form as the Windsor De Luxe models, but on the longer wheelbase. Imperials were built as sedans, club coupes, hardtops, convertibles and long-wheelbase cars for most of the early period, and in 1950 there was a special sedan with custom interior.

Perhaps it was the plain styling that gave rise to Chysler's reputation for engineering, which was certainly the company's great strength in the early '50s. A change in the power plant lineup was part of the emphasis on engineering.

The Chrysler Six had been a dominant seller for some years, so its disappearance after 1954 came as a surprise to many. But in reality it was part of a broad-based plan, partly instigated by Keller's successor, Lester Lum "Tex" Colbert.

Colbert set several early goals, among which were the decentralization of divisional management, the total redesign of all passenger cars as soon as possible, and an ambitious program of plant expansion and financing. Giving the divisions freer rein meant that people close to the sales level could take more control in mapping policy. At Chrysler Division, the only market sector available was the top one: DeSoto had staked out the ground below Chrysler.

The hemi-head V8 had arrived in 1951, so the Six was gradually deemphasized. It had taken close to 100,000 sales in 1950, but dropped to 84,000 by 1953 and to 45,000 in 1954.

The hemispherical-head V8, which had a displacement of 331 cubic inches and a bore and stroke of 3¹³⁄₁₆x3⅝ inches, was first offered on the 1951 New Yorker and Imperial models. The hemi-head (not really a new idea at the time), offered exceptionally good volumetric efficiency. It had a lower compression ratio and therefore could use lower-octane fuel than non-hemis could, yet it was capable of producing power equivalent to that of conventional engines.

The hemi was more than ample as a power plant: one early demonstration version achieved 352 bhp on the dynamometer after minor modifications to the camshaft, carburetors and exhaust. Drag racers would later get as much as 1000 horsepower from the hemi. It was, however, complex and costly, requiring double the number of rocker shafts, pushrods and rockers. Its interchangeable heads were heavy and expensive to manufacture. As a result, the hemi was replaced on the '59 Chryslers by a more conventional 383 wedge-head V8; but while it was around, it wrote a great story.

A stock Saratoga hemi would run 0 to 60 in as little as 10 seconds and achieve close to 110 miles per hour flat out. Bill Sterling won the Mexican Road Race stock-car class in a Saratoga and was third overall—behind two Ferraris—in 1951. Chryslers placed high in NASCAR racing, though they were eclipsed by the remarkable Hudson Hornets. Briggs Cunningham began running his outstanding sports cars in European road races, and in 1953 drove his C-5R to third place at Le Mans. He averaged 104.14 mph, against 105.85 mph for the winning Jaguar C-type.

Chrysler engineers had built four special hemis for the 1953 Indianapolis 500, all of which developed over 400 horsepower using Hillborn fuel injection. But a displacement limit prevented the engineers from realizing the power plants' full potential. Then came the Chrysler 300 in 1955, delivering 300 bhp from the stock engine. The car dominated NASCAR racing in 1955-56 and probably would have done so for several years thereafter had the Auto Manufacturers Association not agreed to deemphasize racing.

The 300 was part of Virgil Exner's all-new cars for 1955—the ones that rallied Chrysler from a 100,000-unit year in 1954 to 176,000 units, and finally brought styling up to par with performance. Based on a long line of Ghia-bodied Exner show cars, the '55s were clean and aggressive looking. Their 1956 successors were generally even better—something rare in a face lift during the 1950s. The modestly grilled, gracefully finned Forward Look cars of 1957 were probably Exner's design pinnacle. The '57 Chrysler 300-C was a breathtaking car—big and hairy, yet safe and controllable, and it was available as a convertible for the first time. But the other models were attractive too, and offered numerous trim options.

The 1955 Chrysler 300 at Daytona.

1957 300-C hardtop. Price: $4929.

1957 Dart show car in the age of fins.

For 1955-56, there were actually two two-door hardtops, Nassau and St. Regis, in the Windsor and New Yorker lines. The latter were more conservatively two-toned and offered a slightly better interior. There were six- and nine-passenger Town & Country station wagons from 1958 on, plus the Exner four-door hardtop. A hastily conceived item in 1956, it was pretty in its 1957 form.

The Saratoga returned in '57, and over 37,000 units were sold that year. Saratoga again offered a performance premium—a 295-hp version of the hemi. PowerFlite two-speed automatic transmission had come along in 1953, evolving into a three-speed TorqueFlite by 1957. The three-speed was one of the finest automatics ever built. In 1957, it was controlled by the famous Chrysler push buttons, mounted in a handy pod to the left of the steering wheel.

Chrysler

1958 New Yorker convertible. Price: $4761

1959 Saratoga hardtop, priced at $4026.

The styling of the 1957 Chryslers was superb. But Chrysler's rush to set the styling pace had a negative effect on overall quality. Quality control was also hampered by a series of strikes.

No discussion of Chrysler in the 1950s is complete without a mention of Torsion-Aire ride, which was offered from 1957 onward. Torsion bars were not a new idea—Packard had introduced an excellent four-wheel system in 1955—but Torsion-Aire went a long way toward making big American cars handle decently. This they desperately needed in the mid-1950s. Instead of sending road shocks up into the car like coil or leaf springs did, torsion bars absorbed the force by winding up against their anchor points. The resulting twisting motion eliminated most of the upward force of road irregularities. Unlike Packard, Chrysler put torsion bars on the front wheels only. It's likely that their use had more to do with enlarging engine compartment space than with radically altering the suspension; nevertheless, torsion bars must be regarded as a major step toward improved handling. The fact that they're still present on Chryslers today is an indication that the idea worked.

Partly as a result of buyer dissatisfaction with Chrysler quality and partly because of the recession, 1958 was a terrible year for the division. There was no major styling change to enhance the line's allure. High hopes were pinned on Exner's restyling plans for '59.

The Chryslers of 1959 were less graceful than their predecessors, with soaring tailfins. Yet the fins seemed to solve the sales problem. The "lion-hearted" Chryslers saw close to 70,000 sales in calendar year 1959.

A Windsor convertible was added, but otherwise the 1959 line was the same as the '58: Windsors rode the 122-inch wheelbase that had appeared the year before; the rest of the cars kept the 126-inch wheelbase that had been used since 1955. The new 383 wedge-head engine wasn't as powerful as the hemi, but it was much simpler to build. That engine is another Chrysler invention that survived until modern times. In the New Yorker and 300-E for '59, the wedge-head was bored out to 413 cubic inches and produced up to 380 hp at 5000 rpm.

The 300-E has been unduly criticized as a weakling in comparison to its hemi-powered predecessors, but road tests do not bear this out. The '59 was just as quick as the 300-D before it. With 10.1:1 compression, TorqueFlite and a 3.31:1 rear axle ratio, the E would accelerate from rest to 60 miles an hour in less than 8.5 seconds; in 17.5 seconds, it would be doing 90. But only 690 were built in 1959. That was a record low for the 300 series.

Virgil Exner left in 1962, and Chrysler sold record numbers of cars in the '60s. But many people agree that the cars of the '50s were Chrysler's most exciting models. Collectors gather them in great numbers, and their place in history seems assured.

CHRYSLER AT A GLANCE 1950-1959

Model Year	1950	1951	1952	1953	1954	1955	1956	1957	1958	1959
Price Range, $	2134-5384	2388-6740	2495-7044	2472-7044	2541-7044	2660-4209	2870-4419	3088-5359	3129-5603	3204-5749
Weight Range, Lbs.	3540-5305	3570-5450	3550-5430	3600-5275	3565-5295	3925-4430	3900-4460	3995-4490	3860-4475	3735-4360
Wheelbases, Ins.	125.5-145.5	125.5-145.5	125.5-145.5	125.5-145.5	125.5-145.5	126	126	126	122-126	122-126
6 Cyl Engines, BHP	116	116	119	119	119					
8 Cyl Engines, BHP	135	180	180	180	195-235	188-300	225-340	285-390	290-390	305-380

Clipper

Packard-Clipper Division of Studebaker-Packard Corp., Detroit, Michigan

When marketing wizard James J. Nance became president of Packard in 1952, he immediately began a movement to divorce the medium-priced Packard 200 from the luxury Packard lines, declaring that continued emphasis on cheaper cars after World War II had been "bleeding the Packard name white." The 200 became the Packard Clipper in 1953. For 1956, Nance officially registered Clipper as an individual make. There were separate Packard and Clipper dealer signs, and the factory was renamed Packard-Clipper Division of Studebaker-Packard Corporation. The Packard name appeared nowhere on Clippers except for a tiny script on the deck lid. (Early models didn't even display this.)

Nance's aim was to separate the Clipper still further from Studebaker-Packard for 1957. Clipper was to use the larger Studebaker body shell; Packard was to continue with one of its own. This never materialized, because lenders failed to commit sufficient funds. Nance resigned in August 1956.

Studebaker-Packard got a temporary reprieve by way of a management agreement with Curtiss-Wright Corporation. Curtiss-Wright needed S-P mainly as a tax loss. Under C-W management, the Packard name was saved for 1957's deluxe line of Studebaker-based cars. But, since these were again called Packard Clippers, the Clipper make disappeared.

The 1956 Clipper appeared in De Luxe, Super and Custom series, which shared two body styles and five models. All used a 122-inch-wheelbase chassis and an overhead-valve Packard V8. The 352 cubic-inch powerplant produced 240 horsepower at 4600 rpm in the Super and De Luxe; 275 hp in the Custom. All models used Packard's innovative Torsion Level suspension, although a conventional suspension was available on the bottom-line De Luxe. Clipper options included overdrive transmission ($110), Ultramatic ($199), power steering, power brakes and air conditioning.

1956 Super Panama hardtop. Price: $2916.

1956 De Luxe sedan, priced at $2731.

Clippers were luxuriously trimmed and nicely styled, though their sales volume wasn't sufficient to help the company. The De Luxe sedan was the best seller, at 5715 units. The Custom Constellation hardtop was rarest, selling only 1466 units. Only 2129 sedans were sold. The Super Panama hardtop sold 3999 copies, and the Super sedan sold 5173.

The Clipper as a separate make was a good idea that came too late. Had the firm begun divorcing its lower-priced cars from the Packard name in 1946, when it was benefiting from a huge seller's market, the story of 1956 might have had a happier ending.

CLIPPER AT A GLANCE 1950-1959

Model Year	1950	1951	1952	1953	1954	1955	1956	1957	1958	1959
Price Range, $							2731-3164			
Weight Range, Lbs.							3745-3860			
Wheelbases, Ins.							122			
8 Cyl Engines, BHP							240-275			

Continental

Continental Division of Ford Motor Co., Dearborn, Michigan

The first thing to say about the 1956-60 Continental is that it was not a Lincoln. It was the product of a separate division of Ford, created with the goal of establishing dominance in the highest-priced field, higher even than Cadillac. Only one model was produced for 1956 and 1957: the flawlessly styled and beautifully built Mark II. It was priced at $10,000, and was worth every penny. Yet Ford lost about $1000 on every Mark II sold, because the car was a line leader—more an ego trip than a calculated profit maker. An attempt was made to put Continental into the black with a lower-priced line of cars from 1958 to 1960, but they never sold particularly well. The separate division was gone by 1961, and the Continental name was applied to the new line of four-door hardtops and convertibles designed by Elwood Engel.

Ever since the demise of the old Lincoln Conti-

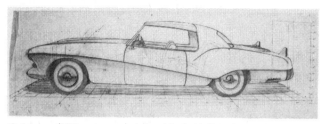

Grisinger/Miller proposal for Mark II Continental.

nental in 1948, Ford had been pressured by dealers and customers to build a successor. In 1953, with profits looking up, the effort was begun. William Clay Ford, younger brother of Henry Ford II, was placed in charge of a Special Products Division to come up with a design. He called in five outside consultants to submit their ideas for comparison.

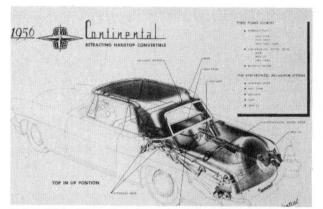

Retractable Mark II hardtop considered for production.

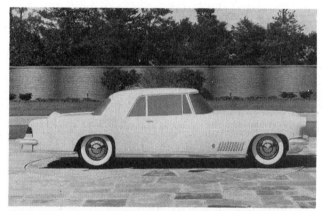

Mark II production prototype. Scallops later dropped.

1956 Continental Mark II. Price: $9695.

The outsiders were a distinguished lot: Walter Buell Ford (no relation), Buzz Grisinger, Reese Miller, Vince Gardner and George Walker. Walker later became Ford's chief of design. Though the consultants came up with several nice ideas, it was no contest. Ford management reviewed 13 different presentations using front, side, rear and three-quarter front views; and unanimously selected the design from John Reinhart, Gordon Buehrig and Bob Thomas of Special Products. Harley F. Copp, chief engineer of the Special Products Division, designed a special chassis frame of steel rails. It dipped low between the wheels to provide high seats without creating too high a roofline. The starkly simple cockpit and dash were inspired by aircraft and locomotive designs. The engines used were specially selected and balanced Lincoln 368 cubic-inch V8s. These power plants, with 4x 3 5/16-inch bore and stroke, produced 285 to 300 horsepower at 4600 rpm. They were connected to Multi-Drive three-speed automatic transmissions and 3.07:1 rear axles. The sleek and timeless coupe measured 218.5 inches overall and rode on a 126-inch wheelbase. It was greeted with wonderment on both sides of the Atlantic, and has been considered one of the all-time great design achievements ever since its debut. It was in a class by itself. Ford had set out to eclipse Cadillac with the Mark II and assumed that it had succeeded. Even the Eldorado Brougham of 1957-58 was chrome-laden kitsch compared to the Continental.

But the euphoria didn't last. Through Continental Division was hoping to add a beautiful four-door berline and perhaps a convertible to the line for 1958, word from the sales department deflated those hopes. The Mark II had not made a difference in actual production, and General Motors was still the leader. A moneyed few were buying Mark IIs, but the car was not influencing those with less cash to buy Lincolns instead of Cadillacs.

Accordingly, a cut in price from the $10,000 of 1956-57 to $6000 or $7000 for 1958 was planned. A Mercury cost expert was brought in, and a new Continental appeared. It was a Lincoln-based giant on a 131-inch wheelbase. It had elongated fenders, garish chrome appliques, huge tailfins and canted headlamps. The new Mark III was available in four versions: sedan, four-door and two-door hardtops,

1958 Mark III Landau sedan. Price: $6072.

and a convertible. The price was $5825 to $6283. The Mark III sold a bit better than the II.

In 1959, a Mark IV arrived. A town car and limousine were added at extraordinary prices. A similar course was taken in 1960 with the Mark V. The Marks then ended, and were replaced by the Lincoln Continental line. Continental Division quietly disappeared. Sales through 1960 were always far above the Mark II's level, because more models were available.

One Ford executive said years later that the Mark II program was, on balance, a tragedy. "For obvious reasons we don't like to talk about it," he said. "What we had going for us in the Mark II was literally a revival of the Duesenberg concept. What we ended up with was something much less — and even that didn't last long . . . It was a project that for a time broke Bill Ford's heart, and I guess you could say that in many ways it broke ours too."

In retrospect, it seems Ford Motor Company agreed with that analysis. When Ford revived the Continental for a third time in 1968, the new model was called Mark III and was touted as the successor to the 1956-57 Mark II. The Marks of 1958-60 were treated as though they had never existed. The Continental has progressed through Mark V again. Whether these recent machines are Lincolns or Continentals is debatable.

But the Mark II was definitely a Continental, in the classic, respected sense of the name. It was one of the world's outstanding motorcars.

CONTINENTAL AT A GLANCE 1950-1959

Model Year	1950	1951	1952	1953	1954	1955	1956	1957	1958	1959
Price Range, $							9695	9966	5825-6283	6598-10,230
Weight Range, Lbs.							4825	4800	4865-5040	4967-6000
Wheelbases, Ins.							126	126	131	131
8 Cyl Engines, BHP							285	300	375	350

Crosley

**Crosley Motors Inc.,
Cincinnati, Ohio**

Powel Crosley Jr. was an innovator. He'd proved that as a young man, by developing and selling a $20 radio at a time when most radios cost five times that much. By 1922, he had become the world's largest manufacturer of radios. He then turned his attention to building and selling refrigerators, and was very successful in that area too.

America was not as receptive to another of Crosley's innovations: a low-cost automobile with an 80-inch wheelbase and an engine made of stamped sheet metal. Crosley began building his lightweight economy car in Richmond, Indiana, in 1939. After the war, he relocated to Cincinnati. A total of 24,871 Crosleys were built in calendar year 1948, but production soon began to plummet. A reviving U.S. economy and increasing family incomes made Crosleys less attractive in the 1950s than they'd been earlier. Only 7043 cars were built by Crosley in 1950; production fell to 4839 in 1951; it sank to 1522 the following year, which marked the end of the make.

The Crosley line of the 1950s comprised a station wagon; a convertible; a sedan; a doorless sports model called the Hot Shot; and the SS, a second sporty model with doors. A business coupe was listed in 1951 and '52, but it doesn't show up in production figures. Prices ranged from $882 for the 1950 SS to $1077 for the 1952 station wagon. These prices put Crosley cars in a class by themselves. Their engineering also was unique.

Power for the tiny cars originally came from an overhead-cam Four with a block made of sheet metal stampings. It displaced 44 cubic inches, had a bore and stroke of 2.5x2.25 inches, produced 26.5 horsepower at 5400 rpm and weighed about 60 pounds. The engine was a modification of a power plant that had been developed during World War II for use in everything from truck refrigerators to Mooney Mite airplanes.

Crosleys used disc brakes from 1949 to 1950—another innovation. They were the first production cars anywhere in the world to use them.

1952 Super Sport owned by Juanita Cummins.

Both the engine and the brakes, which seemed like excellent ideas at the time they were introduced, later proved troublesome and were replaced with conventional designs. The sheet-metal engine—crimped and spot-welded, then copper brazed—suffered from electrolysis; the cylinders became riddled with holes and the engines required rebuilding. The disc brakes quickly deteriorated when exposed to road salt. Crosley went to a cast-iron engine block in 1949 and replaced the disc brakes with drums in 1950. These problems had hurt the company, so much so that potential buyers ignored the good points of Crosleys.

One of those good points was the Hot Shot's racing performance. In 1951, riding on a new 85-inch wheelbase and powered by the cast-iron engine, the sporty little car could do a rollicking 90 miles per hour. It held the road well with its I-beam, semi-elliptical springs in front and coils and quarter elliptics at the rear. A Hot Shot won the Index of Performance at Sebring that year.

Buyers were not impressed. Production of Crosley cars came to an end in mid-1952 and the company merged with General Tire and Rubber Company. Innovator Powel Crosley had spent an estimated $3 million of his own money on the little cars—on ideas whose time had not yet come.

CROSLEY AT A GLANCE 1950-1959

Model Year	1950	1951	1952	1953	1954	1955	1956	1957	1958	1959
Price Range, $	882-984	943-1077	943-1077							
Weight Range, Lbs.	1175-1403	1184-1403	1175-1403							
Wheelbases, Ins.	80, 85	80, 85	80, 85							
4 Cyl Engines, BHP	26.5	26.5	26.5							

Cunningham

**B.S. Cunningham Co.,
West Palm Beach, Florida**

Many car enthusiasts dream of building their own automobiles. Wealthy sportsman Briggs Swift Cunningham did just that from 1951 to 1955, producing the fastest cars in America and very nearly winning Le Mans with one of them. The prototype of the series was the 1951 C-1, which rode on a 105-inch wheelbase. It had been beautifully styled by Cunningham and his team, fully instrumented and sumptuously upholstered with leather on comfortable bucket seats. The C-2R series followed, using both open and closed body designs. Both cars were powered by the Chrysler hemi-head V8 that produced 180 horsepower in stock form; but Cunningham got much more out of it than that, as much as 300 bhp. The C-2Rs failed at Le Mans in 1951, however. They were too heavy and the engines wouldn't run well on low-octane French gasoline.

The C-3 of 1953-55 was Cunningham's "volume" car. This $10,000 grand tourer used its predecessors' tubular frame and race-proven suspension. Its coupe body was built by Michelotti, then of the Vignale coachbuilding firm. The C-3 was a beautiful car. It and Studebaker's 1953 Starliner were the only American cars included on the list of the World's Ten Best Cars.

Back at Le Mans for 1952, Cunningham entered three copies of his new C-4R. They were each lighter by 1000 pounds than the C-2R, rode on a 100-inch wheelbase and were powered by a 325-hp hemi. Two of the three cars eventually dropped out, but Cunningham himself drove the other car to fourth place overall, behind two Mercedes-Benz racers and a Nash-Healey. He broke the distance record in the 5-to-8-liter class. In 1953, two of the C-4Rs were back, along with a C-5R. The newer model was an aggressive-looking sports car with

1951 Cunningham C-1 prototype.

torsion-bar suspension, Hallibrand knock-off wheels and Al-Fin brake drums of 17-inch diameter. It was timed at 156 mph and finished third, behind two D-type Jaguars. The Jags weren't necessarily faster, but they benefited from new disc brakes. The two C-4Rs placed seventh and tenth.

Cunningham raced a Ferrari in 1954 while his C-6R was being built. The debut of the C-6R the following year was anticlimactic. Powered by a 3-liter Offenhauser engine, it lacked sufficient endurance for the 24-hour race, and Cunningham did not finish. After that, Cunningham quit racing. "If you lost more than $50,000 a year for five consecutive years, you were classified as a hobby by the tax people," he said recently. The race rules were against him: there was nothing in America that was competitive in the new 3-liter category. Briggs went on to a fine career of racing other people's cars. His Cunningham effort is respected. He came very close to winning Le Mans with an all-American car, long before Ford decided to sponsor one with its millions.

Briggs Cunningham today, with his C-5R.

De Soto

De Soto Division of Chrysler Corp., Detroit, Michigan

De Soto's production declined throughout the 1950s, to barely more than a trickle by the end of the decade. Its 1961 models, hastily curtailed just after announcement, were its last.

A realignment of Chrysler Corporation's traditional approach to marketing hurt De Soto. Prior to the realignment, there were three types of corporate retail agencies: they sold either De Sotos, Dodges or Chryslers; and each had a Plymouth franchise as well. But this scene began to change in 1955 when Imperial became a separate make, forcing Chrysler Division to expand downward. That it did, and with success. At the same time, Dodge was reaching upward, tempting De Soto buyers with lower-priced models of basically the same size and with similar performance. De Soto found it difficult to lure many buyers away from Chryslers, which had a better name, so De Soto's demise was inevitable. But while this all was happening, De Soto built some of its finest cars.

In the early '50s, De Sotos were all six-cylinder cars. They used engines of 236.7 to 250.6 cubic inches, L-head Sixes that provided up to 116 horsepower in the Deluxe and Custom series. The Deluxe was a utilitarian car, available as a sedan, club coupe and Carry-all sedan. The Custom series offered wagons instead of Carry-alls, a hardtop and a convertible, and two long-wheelbase sedans.

In 1950, the cars were boxy, and had more chrome in front than perhaps any other Chrysler product. Virgil Exner brought in a somewhat sleeker style in 1951, when the famous "teeth" appeared in De Soto grilles.

For 1952, De Soto introduced the hemi-head FireDome, a 276.1 cubic-inch V8 based on the larger Chrysler version. It developed 160 hp at 4400 rpm and put De Soto in the horsepower race. Immediately, the FireDome Eight series accounted for 45,000 sales. The Custom and Deluxe series were combined in 1953 to form the PowerMaster Six series, which comprised a sedan, club coupe, hardtop, wagon and long sedan. The PowerMaster didn't fare well in competition with the eight-cylinder FireDomes: by the end of '53, FireDomes

1950 Custom wood wagon, priced at $3113.

1953 FireDome long sedan, $3559.

1951 Custom Sportsman hardtop. Price: $2781.

1953 De Soto Adventurer I show car.

were outselling PowerMasters by a margin of two to one. Both the PowerMaster Six and the Fire-Dome V8 series included Sportsman hardtops, very popular cars.

Model year 1954 marked the debut of the PowerFlite two-speed automatic transmission. Through that year, De Sotos came with the three-speed manual transmission standard. Fluid Drive was the major gearbox option at a price of $130, followed by overdrive at $96. That year also marked the end of the PowerMaster Six and the long-wheelbase sedans. The brilliantly engineered, good-looking 1955 models, the FireDome and the new top-of-the-line FireFlite, came with 291 cubic-inch V8s. The V8 developed 185 hp in the FireDome and 200 hp in the FireFlite.

Those 1955 cars, with their attractive two-toned color panels,''gullwing'' dash and highly chromed front end, came just in time to temporarily save the division. Sales had been very poor in 1954—a nightmare period for Chrysler Corporation.

No '55 Chrysler product was really sedate in appearance, and the De Sotos were possibly the most glittery of all. They appealed to buyers and sold well, putting the De Soto over the 100,000 mark. The 126-inch De Soto wheelbase was shared with Chrysler. The FireDome series offered a cheap Special hardtop at $110 less than the Sportsman; the Coronado sedan led the FireFlite series at a $100 premium over the $2800 standard sedan. The Coronado is a minor collector's item today. Its significance in history results from the fact that it joined with Dodge and Buick in the introduction of three-tone paint jobs during 1955.

Horsepower went up to 230 and 255 in 1956. The teeth were yanked out of the grille and were replaced with a wire mesh. Unreadable gold-on-white instruments appeared, and De Sotos grew tailfins with the rest of the Chrysler line. Generally, this face lift produced uglier cars. A highlight, however, was the new limited-edition De Soto Adventurer, a gold-bedecked supercar that came in two-door hardtop form only and listed at $3728, f.o.b. Detroit. It was equipped with a 341 cubic-inch, 320-hp engine. It was part of the wild Chrysler performance assortment that also included the 300-B, Plymouth Fury and Dodge D-500.

One other introduction for 1956 was De Soto's first four-door hardtop as part of the FireDome series. It was called Seville. De Soto's Seville appeared just as Cadillac was adopting that name for its two-door hardtop Eldorado, but no legal entanglements developed. Chrysler just dropped Seville by the end of the year, after Cadillac apparently demonstrated that it had rights to the name.

De Soto fared extremely well in 1956, while other Chrysler divisions suffered extensive production cutbacks. And 1957 proved to be another successful year. The new, low-cost FireSweep built on the 122-inch Chrysler Windsor wheelbase joined the two upper lines in a last effort to extend De Soto's

1954 FireDome convertible. Price: $3144.

1955 FireFlite Sportsman hardtop, $2939.

1956 Adventurer hardtop, priced at $3728.

De Soto Indianapolis 500 pace car in 1956.

De Soto

market downward. The FireSweep helped; you could buy one for only $2777 (the cheapest Fire-Dome was $2958), and there was a full line of sedans, hardtops and wagons available to choose from.

In 1957, De Soto came as near as it ever did to passing Chrysler in production, ending up less than 1000 units behind. These were big, heavy, powerful cars. The two upper series used a V8 that displaced 341 cubic inches and produced up to 295 horse-power. (The FireSweep engine was more con-servative, displacing 325 cubic inches and produc-ing about 260 hp.) The Adventurer soft-top made its debut, offering 345 horsepower.

Of all the Exner finned fantasies that made their debut that year, the De Sotos were the cleanest. Smooth rear panels, attractive taillights, simple but

pleasant molding along the sides, and a front bumper that was unique to the division all helped to give the '57 De Sotos the styling of a classic.

Yet, as good as the De Sotos of '57 looked, the division would not be able to survive on looks alone. From a production level of 117,747 units in calendar year 1957, De Soto fell to 36,556 the fol-lowing year—the lowest production for the division since 1938. The recession, a reputation for poor quality and unwise marketing decisions all contrib-uted to De Soto's downward spiral in 1958. Chrysler Division wasn't doing much better.

The De Sotos for 1958 were basically the same as the 1957s, although the cars did get a mild face lift. The grille became busier, and all cars came with four lights. (As of 1957, some states still had not legalized "quadrilights," so De Soto fenders were designed to accept either one or two pair.) Wagons and Sportsman hardtops proliferated along with four-door sedans. With the addition of a FireSweep model, De Soto offered no fewer than four convert-ibles. The Adventurer, priced at $4369 in 1958, was

1957 De Soto Adventurer two-door hardtop, $3997.

1958 FireDome sedan, priced at $3085.

1957 FireFlite Sportsman hardtop, $3614.

1958 Adventurer convertible, $4369.

1959 FireFlite Sportsman hardtop, $3888.

the most expensive De Soto in history. That price put it up in Chrysler New Yorker territory, but Chrysler's corresponding 300-D cost $1300 more than the De Soto soft-top.

In 1955, De Sotos were extremely fast cars. Fast-shifting TorqueFlite automatic transmission and torsion-bar suspension made them some of the most road-worthy cars in the country. A De Soto FireDome with Turboflash V8 and the optional 305-hp setup could accelerate from 0 to 60 in 7.7 seconds and to 80 in 13.5 seconds, and it could reach 115 mph with little strain. De Soto's performance orientation affected the Adventurer, also. It was available in '58 with 355 horsepower.

De Soto said the towering tailfins of 1957-61 "added stability at speed," but this was advertising propaganda: they did nothing from an aerodynamic standpoint, but they did make the cars look dramatically different from the opposition. De Soto tailfins reached their height in 1959. What followed after that was the beginning of the end. However, by the time fins finally disappeared, De Soto had departed too.

De Soto had joined the switch to wedge-head engines in '58. For 1959 FireSweeps used the 361 cubic-inch unit, and other models got the potent 383. Maximum horsepower—standard on the Adventurer—was 350 hp at 5000 rpm. The wedgeheads gave little to the hemis in acceleration.

As before, there was a wide choice of hardtops, wagons, sedans and convertibles. The Adventurer became a volume series in 1959, and sales improved slightly to 41,423 for the 12 months. Yet this was hardly the kind of volume that De Soto had sustained earlier in the decade, holding on to 12th place in the industry and serving as a major profit maker for Chrysler Corporation. The handwriting was on the wall.

De Soto show cars vied with those of the Chrysler label in the '50s. They were built mainly by Ghia to Exner's designs. Adventurer I was the first, part of Exner's early series which began with the 1951 Chrysler K-310. Produced in 1954, the Adventurer I rode a shortened 111-inch wheelbase and accommodated four passengers. Its off-white coupe body was fitted with outside exhausts, wire wheels and full instrumentation. It came closer than any other Exner special to production. "Had it been mass-produced," Exner said, "it would have been the first four-passenger sports car made in this country. It was better than a two-plus-two, and of course it had the De Soto hemi. It was my favorite car always, and I owned it for three years and kept it at home."

Adventurer II followed in 1955. This conventional-wheelbase, four-passenger coupe was designed more by Ghia's craftsmen than Exner. It was painted deep red and fitted with wire wheels. It had no bumper. Adventurer II lacked the sleek continuity of styling that its predecessor had, and was not seriously considered for production.

De Soto struggled on for another two years, with its production steadily dropping. By 1961 the De Soto name had faded from passenger cars.

DE SOTO AT A GLANCE 1950-1959

Model Year	1950	1951	1952	1953	1954	1955	1956	1957	1958	1959
Price Range, $	1996-3199	2235-3586	2339-3754	2364-3559	2364-3559	2498-3151	2678-3728	2777-4272	2819-4369	2904-4749
Weight Range, Lbs.	3450-4400	3475-4395	3435-4370	3480-4270	3505-4305	3805-4115	3780-4070	3645-4290	3660-4295	3625-4170
Wheelbases, Ins.	125.5, 139.5	125.5, 139.5	125.5, 139.5	125.5, 139.5	125.5, 139.5	126	126	122, 126	122, 126	122, 126
6 Cyl Engines, BHP	112	116	116	116	116					
8 Cyl Engines, BHP			160	160	170	188, 200	230-320	245-345	280-355	295-350

Dodge

Dodge Division of Chrysler Corp., Hamtramck, Michigan

Like Chevrolet's, Dodge's image was transformed in the '50s. Dodges began as stodgy six-bangers, but soon became track stars. Dodge styling kept pace with performance. The division had its ups and downs in sales, however, for it deserted one kind of buyer to acquire another.

Dodge performed a major face lift on the three-box styling (one box on top of two others) of 1950. It added a new Diplomat hardtop and Gyro-Matic drive, an improvement on standard Fluid Drive that eliminated gear changing. All cars were powered by the sturdy 103-horsepower flathead Six. This 230.2 cubic-inch engine with bore and stroke of 3.3x4.8 inches would serve Dodge through the decade. Two basic series were fielded. The D33 Wayfarer, including a winsome sport convertible at $1745, was priced just above the more expensive Plymouths. The D34 series comprised Meadowbrook and Coronet sedans; and Coronet wagons, coupes, convertibles and hardtops. Through 1952, Coronet would also offer long-wheelbase sedans, Dodge's heaviest cars, for taxi and limousine purposes.

There's not much to say about Dodge styling of the early '50s. It was pretty dull. Though dull, Dodges represented a step up in prestige for Plymouth owners in those years, and the cars served Dodge well. The division built over 300,000 cars in 1950 and again in 1951, rising to sixth place in the industry in '51. Dodge held onto sixth in 1952 by building only 260,000 cars, but dropped back to eighth in 1953 even though production reached 293,000 units.

Without a switch in wheelbases, the styling became smoother and sleeker for 1951-52 than it had been in '50. A lower grille opening, clean flanks and faired-in taillights gave the cars a new look. The model lineup for 1951-52 remained exactly as it had been in 1950. Wayfarers set the price pace; Coronets supplied the widest variety of body styles; and Meadowbrook filled the gap between them with a four-door sedan. The cars were changed only slightly for '52—the grille bar immediately above the bumper was painted.

In 1953, a restyling was accompanied by the Red Ram V8 and the first Dodge performance cars. The Red Ram displaced 241.3 cubic inches, had a 3.44x3.25-inch bore and stroke, and first produced 140 horsepower—though it was capable of much more than that. It was essentially a scaled-down version of the 331 cubic-inch Chrysler hemi, introduced in 1951. Chrysler had long been experimenting with hemispherical combustion chambers, and was now cashing in on what had been

1950 Wayfarer Sport Roadster, $1745.

1950 Coronet station wagon, $2883.

1952 Wayfarer coupe. Price: $1904.

learned. The hemi's advantages included smoother manifolding and porting, larger valves set farther apart, improved thermal efficiency, plenty of room for water passages, a more central spark plug location and low heat rejection into coolant. Its main disadvantage was its cost: engine for engine, Red Rams were more expensive to build than Chevy 265s, for example.

The 1953 Dodges were among the first production cars styled by Virgil Exner, who had come to Chrysler from Studebaker a few years earlier. Riding on wheelbases of 114 to 119 inches, they were light cars that handled well. They were known for economy as well as performance. A V8 Dodge scored 23.4 miles per gallon in the '53 Mobilgas Economy Run; the same year, other V8s broke 196 AAA stock car records at Bonneville, and Danny Eames drove one to a record 102.62 mph at El Mirage dry lake in California. Dodge's V8 was a low-displacement, high-efficiency power plant; unique in its hemi-head construction, reliable and very strong.

Detail changes only were made for '54. However, a new, luxurious Royal series appeared and was joined in the middle of the year by the Royal 500 convertible named for the Indianapolis race. Dodge had paced the Indiana classic that year, and a round of pace-car replicas seemed like a good idea. Included in the 500 package at only $2632 were Kelsey-Hayes chrome wire wheels, a "continental" spare tire, special ornamentation and a 150-bhp Red Ram V8. Dealers could even specify a four-barrel Offenshauser manifold which must have made the 500 a screamer, though Chrysler never quoted its actual horsepower.

Of the 1799 Royal convertibles Dodge sold in 1954, only 701 were Royal 500s, but the performance package was far more successful than the sales figure suggests. The division had established itself as the performance team at Chrysler, and Dodges continued to roll up victories. Lincoln is famous for its dominance of the Mexican Road Race in these years, but what is not widely known is that Dodge also overwhelmed its Medium Stock class—taking 1-2-3-4-6-9 positions in the 1954 marathon.

Those racing successes helped to boost sales. In a generally poor year for Chrysler products, the '54 Dodge sold well. The division came back with another major restyling that was mainly the work of Exner staff member Murray Baldwin. The '55s were set on a new 120-inch wheelbase. Coronets, Royals and Custom Royals offered engine options of up to 193 hp. They were much larger cars, but were conservatively styled and really well built.

In 1956, Exner's wonders all grew tailfins. Dodge was no exception. Powerflite automatic transmission, which had first arrived on Dodges with gear lever control in 1954, was introduced with push buttons in '56. New styling details and new interiors were coupled with a new engine, the optional D-500 V8. It displaced 315 cubic inches and developed a hefty 260 bhp at 4400 rpm. Dodge also unveiled its first four-door hardtop Lancer, in all three series. In a declining year for the industry, the division built only 205,727 cars but still managed to hold onto eighth place. The following year, with torsion-bar suspension and new styling again,

1954 Royal sedan, priced at $2373.

1954 Royal convertible, $2632.

1955 Custom Royal Lancer hardtop, $2543.

1955 Custom Royal sedan, $2473.

Dodge

Dodge climbed to seventh place and built nearly 300,000 units.

Exner's Forward Look styling was new from the ground up for 1957, and hadn't progressed to extremes yet. Dodges that year were smoothly styled, aggressive-looking cars with massive bumper-grilles, lots of glass and still more power. An array of hemi engines, ranging from the mild 325 that delivered 245 hp to the top D-500's 354 that delivered 340 hp, offered performance enthusiasts plenty. Even the old Six was increased in horsepower to 138 hp.

Dodge did not follow Chrysler, De Soto and Plymouth with a limited-edition "supercar" in 1957.

Instead, it offered the D-500 package across the board, even on the plain Coronet two-door sedans. All D-500s were equipped with stiff shocks, stiff springs, and torsion bars for what *Motor Trend* called "close liaison with the road." The soft ride of conventional Chrysler cars was passed up in favor of firm settings that put D-500s at the top of their class in handling. And with the 245-hp engine, the car ran 0 to 60 in 9.4 seconds in the Magazine's tests. The D-500 continued in 1958-59, but its expensive hemi was replaced with a wedge-head V8. Fitted with fuel injection for 1958, the 361 cubic-inch wedge would produce 333 hp at 4800 rpm —the highest power offered by Dodge that model year.

Dodges rode 122-inch wheelbases in 1957, and continued with the same bodies for 1958 and 1959. The '58s got a mild but attractive face lift: the adoption of four headlamps, and a less massive

1956 Royal Lancer hardtop, $2543.

1958 Custom Royal Lancer hardtop, $3071.

1957 Custom Royal Lancer convertible, $3146.

1957 Custom Royal Lancer four-door hardtop, $2991.

Swivel seats, popular '59 Dodge feature.

1959 Sierra station wagon, priced at $3103.

frontispiece. The model lineup was generally unchanged, but the Regal series made its debut in February. Regal, an ultraluxurious two-door Lancer hardtop, was priced at $3245.

Fuel injection was a short-lived venture, not marked by wild success. Few buyers opted for the setup. More popular were the conventional Dodge V8s which ranged up to 305 hp. The old flat-head Six was still around, but was relegated to only the Coronet series and was not a wise buy, according to one tester. "It could be pretty much of a white elephant when you go to sell it," he said. Dodge itself was somewhat of a white elephant in 1958, a disastrous year. Production plunged to 114,206 for the 12-month period, barely enough to beat out ailing Studebaker-Packard. Dodge management remained calm—it was, after all, an abnormally poor year—and rebounded with a restyled 1959 line composed of the same basic models. Sure enough, the division built nearly 200,000 cars again in '59 for its traditional eighth-place finish.

Exner's fins went wild in 1959 throughout most of Chrysler Corporation's lineup, but they remained modest on the Dodge. The Dodge front end was given a new look, the interior was revised, and several interesting options were offered. Dodge and its companion divisions offered the popular swivel seat, a semi-bucket affair that pivoted outward as the door opened. The twin four-barrel 383 cubic-inch V8 produced Dodge's top 1959 horsepower—345 at 5000 rpm. Also available were 326 and 361 cubic-inch wedges, and the flat-head Six was marketed for the last time. Incidentally, the D-500 engines weren't cheap. The 383 with four-barrel cost $304 extra; the Super version with twin four-barrel cost $446. The engines were gas hogs, but that was an age of 30-cent gasoline. People were willing to spend extra money on the engines and gas to get the added performance.

Exner's Dodge show cars are worth mention. The first was the Firearrow roadster. At first it was just a mock-up, but was made road-ready for 1954. In late 1954 came a Firearrow sport coupe and convertible. The latter inspired the limited-production Dual-Ghia. The Firearrow coupe was aerodynamically stable, and achieved 143.44 mph on the Chrysler Proving Grounds banked oval.

Another show car was 1955's Dodge La Femme, a Custom Royal Lancer two-door hardtop that was painted pink and upholstered in white. Many custom accoutrements were featured, including a folding umbrella and fitted handbag that rested in the backs of the front seats. La Femme was back again on the 1956 show route, and was all the rage. It stood a chance of seeing serious production for awhile, but no more than a handful were produced.

DODGE AT A GLANCE 1950-1959

Model Year	1950	1951	1952	1953	1954	1955	1956	1957	1958	1959
Price Range, $	1629-2883	1813-2934	1904-3082	1983-2528	1983-3031	2013-2761	2194-2913	2370-3670	2449-3354	2516-3439
Weight Range, Lbs.	3095-4045	3175-3935	3050-3935	3085-3480	3120-3660	3235-3730	3250-3715	3400-4030	3360-4035	3375-4020
Wheelbases, Ins.	115-137.5	115-137.5	115-137.5	114-119	114-119	120	120	122	122	122
6 Cyl Engines, BHP	103	103	103	103	110	123	131	138	138	135
8 Cyl Engines, BHP				140	140, 150	175, 193	189-260	245-340	252-333	255-345

Edsel

Edsel Division of Ford Motor Co., Dearborn, Michigan

Was it a comedy of errors, or a good idea at the time? The Edsel was both—proof that even giant multinational corporations make mistakes. "Its aim was right," says a prominent auto historian, "but the target moved." That is true.

When the Edsel was being developed back in 1955, the field of cars in the lower-medium price range was booming. Pontiac, Buick and Dodge were producing nearly two million vehicles for this sector. But the Edsel appeared in 1958, and by then the market had bottomed out. New-car sales were in a slump generally and the market penetration of medium-price cars dropped from 25 percent to about 18 percent. Edsel Division started with a goal of 100,000 cars for model year 1958. It produced 54,607 cars for '58 by the end of calendar year 1957, but from there it was all downhill. In calendar 1958, only 26,563 Edsels were built. Only 29,677 were built in 1959. The line disappeared for good by the end of November 1959.

The Edsel was never intended to bear Edsel Ford's name, but got it because nothing else worked. Ford had recruited poet Marianne Moore in the naming project. She came up with some stunners, including "Mongoose Civique," "Turcotinga" and "Utopian Turtletop." Ranger, Pacer, Corsair and Citation were the top finishers of the 6000 names considered by the ad agency. Ernie Breech, Ford Motor Company's chairman of the board, didn't like any of them. When told that the Ford Family was against calling the car Edsel, Breech replied, "I'll take care of Henry." And he did.

Ranger and Pacer came on a 116 to 118-inch wheelbase. Corsair and Citation rode on a 124-inch wheelbase and offered a line of hardtops, two- and four-door sedans, convertibles and station wagons spanning a price range of $2519 to $3801, roughly about $500 downstream of comparable Mercurys. Along with their unique horse-collar grille and nar-

1958 Citation four-door hardtop, $3615.

row horizontal taillights, they featured numerous offbeat devices: "Teletouch" buttons for the automatic transmission, which were recessed in the steering wheel hub; rotating drum speedometer; stand-up hood ornament; and huge wraparound bumpers. Ranger and Pacer used the Ford body; Corsair and Citation used the Mercury. The latter two models were limited to two- and four-door hardtops, and the $3801 Citation convertible.

Two V8 engines were offered. The 361 cubic-inch 303 horsepower engine was used in the smaller models and station wagons; the 410 cubic-inch, 345-hp power plant was installed in the Corsair/Citation. Edsels were very fast cars, especially when equipped with the big engine.

For 1959, with sales dropping to the basement level, the lineup was radically cut. Only Rangers, Corsairs and Station Wagons were offered on a 120-inch wheelbase, and a 223 six-cylinder engine became optional on Rangers and wagons. The Corsair line disappeared for 1960, leaving only a handful of Ranger models before Ford threw in the towel.

The Edsel was probably Ford's worst mistake of the '50s. Although the blunder cost a lot of money, it was not a crippling one. Ford took the blow and soon recovered.

EDSEL AT A GLANCE 1950-1959

Model Year	1950	1951	1952	1953	1954	1955	1956	1957	1958	1959
Price Range, $									2519-3801	2629-3072
Weight Range, Lbs.									3724-4311	3547-3842
Wheelbases, Ins.									116-124	120
6 Cyl Engines, BHP										145
8 Cyl Engines, BHP									303-345	200-303

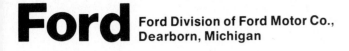

Ford

Ford Division of Ford Motor Co., Dearborn, Michigan

The spinner-nosed 1949-50 Ford was designed in part by Studebaker. Styling was thrown open to many designers, one of whom was Dick Caleal. Caleal approached his friends Robert Bourke and Holden Koto at Studebaker for help in the quarter-scale clay model. In Mrs. Caleal's kitchen the three finished the clay; they baked it, under protest, in her oven. The model was accepted by design chief George Walker and Ford management with little change and became the new '49 Ford. Things sometimes happened that way in the 1950s.

The 1950-53 Fords offered Sixes and a flat-head V8. The latter displaced 239.4 cubic inches. The V8 became popular with hot-rodders and gave Ford a performance edge over Chevrolet and Plymouth. By 1953, the flat-head was pumping out 110 horsepower at 3800 rpm. Ford changed from the flat-head Six to an overhead-valve Six in 1952. From 1951 on, all these engines were accompanied by an optional two-speed Ford-O-Matic shiftless transmission. Ford had tried unsuccessfully to buy Studebaker's first-rate automatic for the '50 model year.

Through these early years of the decade the company experienced a revival, moving ahead of Chrysler into the number two spot. Ford offered a series of interesting cars that sold well.

A special confection for 1950-51 was the V8 Crestliner. This $1779 special-edition two-door was distinguished by a vivid two-tone color panel on its sides and a padded vinyl top. Only 26,304 Crestliners were sold before the series was canceled in 1952, but the wildly colored cars remain collector's items to this day. The rest of the line was divided between DeLuxes and Customs. There were Sixes and V8s, sedans and coupes, Custom wagons, and the Custom V8 convertible. Ford's styling in 1950-51 was rather high and wide by comparison to archrival Chevy's, but was better than Plymouth's. Ford built over one million cars in calendar 1950, the highest total since 1930.

In 1951, the same basic styling produced the hardtop Victoria in the Custom V8 range. This neat alteration of the two-door coupe sold much better than the Crestliner-110,286 units to be exact. Restyling came in 1952. Walker produced the lines that were to form the basis of Fords for the next several years. His cars were lower and wider; their 115-inch wheelbase was longer than that of the 1950-51 models. Mainline and Customline now became the standard and deluxe model names. The Crestliner became a V8 top-of-the-line series comprising Victoria hardtop, Sunliner convertible, and the posh Country Squire station wagon. This was

1950 Custom Deluxe Crestliner, priced at $1779.

1951 Custom V8 Tudor, priced at $1699.

1952 Crestliner Sunliner convertible, $2214.

the first all-steel Ford wagon, with wood decal trim.

Though 1953 was Ford's Golden Anniversary year, no significant changes were made in the line except for an increase in prices. Ford Division built 1.2 million cars that year—an output that was bettered one year later with 1 4 million and shattered

Ford

again in 1955 with 1.8 million cars. Ford was closing in on Chevy, though it was straining its dealers to do so. A Ford could be bought at "less than cost" in 1953-54 as the "Ford Blitz" reached its peak. Chevrolet was not seriously damaged by the onslaught—but the independents were. Unable to discount as much, Studebaker, American Motors and Kaiser-Willys were hit hard. The blitz is generally considered one of the most important factors in the mid-1950s decline of the independents.

Ford made headlines again in 1954, when it introduced its new overhead-valve, Y-block V8 engine of 130 horsepower. It was the hottest engine in the low-priced field. Together with 1954's ball-joint front suspension, the Y-block greatly narrowed the gap in engineering between expensive and inexpensive cars. Though it displaced 239 cubic inches, exactly the same as its flat-head predecessor, the V8 was entirely different in bore and stroke: it was oversquare at 3.63x3.30 inches. Though it had a 7.2:1 compression ratio, the engine could go up to 12:1 if required.

In the styling department, 1954 was the same story as 1953, with one important addition: the Crestline Skyliner hardtop, with a novel front roof section made of transparent plastic. The Skyliner concept was developed by interior styling director L. David Ash. Its contemporary counterpart is today's moonroof, though the moonroofs are made of glass and cover a smaller area.

The 1955 Fords, bearing some resemblance to the 1952-54 models, were good designs. They were clean and highly chromed, with a rakish look of motion. Frank Hershey was the man in charge of the 1955 styling. Hershey also gets most of the credit for the Thunderbird, one of the most important Fords in history.

The two-seat Thunderbird was a spectacular-looking car then, and still is now. The car was the brainchild of division General Manager Lewis D. Crusoe. He'd gone to a Paris auto show and had come back wondering why Ford didn't have a snazzy sports car in its lineup. Hershey's T-Bird, priced at only $2944 for 1955, was the result. Ford had bored its Y-block V8 out to 272 cubic inches for the 1955 line; for the T-Bird, it was bored out still more to 292 to produce nearly 200 horsepower. Compared to Chevrolet's Corvette, the more civilized Thunderbird was a raging success. Ford sold

1953 Customline Six sedan, $1783.

1956 Thunderbird. Price: $2944.

1954 Crestline V8 Country Squire, $2415.

1955 Fairlane V8 Crown Victoria, $2302.

16,155 copies of the 1955 edition; 15,631 of the 1956; and 21,380 of the 1957. Yet, almost before the two-seater came out, Ford's styling department was working on a four-seat Thunderbird for introduction in 1958.

Ford retained its basic line of cars—Mainline, Customline, Fairlane, Station Wagon—for 1956. In that year, Ford tried to make a selling point of safety. The '56 package included a dished steering wheel, break-away rearview mirror and crashproof door locks as standard on all models; padded dash and sun visors cost $16 extra, and factory-installed seat belts cost $9. The public took to safety in a modest way early in the model year. But the rush to equip cars with seat belts overtaxed Ford's supplier, and only 20 percent of the cars were actually so fitted. Ford continued to stress such features. However, when Ford failed to catch Chevrolet in 1956, a lot of dealers said performance was more important than safety.

An interesting 1955-56 model was the Crown Victoria, developed from the 1954 Skyliner. Some Crown Victoria models featured transparent top, divided from the rest of the roof by a broad stainless-steel band. Though it looked like a roll bar, it added little if any strength to the roof. The Crown was dropped for 1957. Altogether, Ford sold 13,344 plastic-roof cars for 1954; 1999 for 1955; and only 603 for 1956. Though attractive, the models were expensive—$2507 in '56—and the plastic roof made them hot on a summer day.

Ford met dealer demand with the restyled '57s, offering a vast array of V8 engines from the 272 cubic-inch, 190-hp "300" power plant on up to the Thunderbird's supercharged 312 V8 of 300 hp. The cars grew only slightly, to wheelbases of 116 and 118 inches, but the model lineup was drastically rearranged. There were Customs, including a business sedan; Custom 300s; Fairlanes; Fairlane 500s, including a Sunliner convertible and a Retractable Hardtop convertible; and Station Wagons. All were available with six-cylinder or V8 power. The wagon series comprised no fewer than 10 versions: six-cylinder and V8 two-door Ranch Wagons and four-door Country Sedans, the deluxe Country Squire and Del Rio. The new styling was particularly simple for the period. It featured a clean, rectangular full-width grille; rakish side molding; and tiny tailfins. It was a good year for Ford. Some statisticians showed the division ahead of Chevrolet for the first time since 1935, but the final tabulation indicated Chevy ahead by a mere 130 cars. Alas, this was the last year for the two-seat Thunderbird. Radically face-lifted from 1956, it sported emphatic tailfins, and a large combination bumper and grille. Priced at $3408, the T-Bird was still an attractive buy.

The Skyliner retractable hardtop was unique. This mid-1957 introduction was based on earlier developmental engineering by Continental Division. (A Mark II retractable was considered, but not

1956 Fairlane Town Victoria. $2249, $2349.

1957 Fairlane 500, two-door: $2339, $2439.

1957 Custom 300 Tudor sedan: $1991, $2205.

produced.) Ford sold 20,766 of the retractables in 1957, but production tapered off quickly. Only 14,713 of the 1958 version and 12,915 of the 1959 were produced. The Skyliner was complicated and expensive: in '57, the retractable cost $350 more than a standard convertible.

Ford settled for a face lift in 1958, using a bumper-grille based on the '57 Thunderbird, and quad headlights. The cheaper of the two Custom series was dropped. Thunderbird appeared with a completely revised, four-seat body. It was available as a hardtop ($3631) or convertible ($3929).

1957 Thunderbird. Price: $3408.

1958 Skyliner. Price: $3163.

1957 Country Squire wagon: $2684-2789.

1959 Ford Galaxie Prototype.

A recession had slowed car sales. Chevrolet, which had restyled its line, was stung. Ford sold fewer cars than Chevrolet, but hadn't invested as much money in them, and was still able to keep production over a million units. The new Thunderbird proved that the buying public wanted four seats. About 38,000 T-Birds were sold.

In 1959, Chevrolet restyled again. The radically finned models didn't strike the public's fancy as well as Chevrolet had hoped they would. Ford passed Chevy by a solid 100,000 units. The '59 Fords used the same old body. Though updated, it was still conservative. Bizarre two-toning and radical fins were avoided in favor of a squared-off grille with floating starlike ornaments, and simple side molding. A new Galaxie series was added. The broad range of Galaxies included sedans, hardtops and a convertible. The standard overhead-valve Six displaced 223 cubic inches and produced a lively 145 horsepower at 4000 rpm; the standard V8 displaced 292 cubic inches and produced 200 hp at 4000 rpm. Optional V8s included the 332 cubic-inch, 225-hp engine (not available on Thunderbirds); and the big 352 power plant of 300 horsepower. Thunderbird buyers could pay $177 extra for the huge Lincoln mill—430 cubic inches, and 350 horsepower at 4400 rpm.

Thunderbird had another superlative year in '59. Close to 70,000 T-Birds were sold, including 57,195 hardtops and 10,261 convertibles. For Ford Motor Company as a whole, '59 justified the strenuous efforts of Henry Ford II and board chairman Ernest Breech. They had assumed control of a third-rate company in 1945, and had turned it into something approaching General Motors' success in less than 15 years.

FORD AT A GLANCE 1950-1959

Model Year	1950	1951	1952	1953	1954	1955	1956	1957	1958	1959
Price Range, $	1332-2262	1424-2253	1526-2384	1537-2403	1548-2415	1606-2944	1748-3151	1879-3408	1967-3929	2132-3979
Weight Range, Lbs.	2965-3510	2960-3550	2984-3640	2987-3609	3021-3684	2980-3605	3032-3638	3141-3689	3171-4069	3283-4064
Wheelbases, Ins.	114	114	115	115	115.5	102, 115.5	102, 115.5	102-118	113-118	113, 118
6 Cyl Engines, BHP	95	95	101	101	115	120	137	144	145	145
8 Cyl Engines, BHP	100	100	110	110	130	162-198	173-225	190-300	205-300	200-350

Frazer Kaiser-Frazer Corp., Willow Run, Michigan

Between the years 1946 and 1951, more than 100,000 Frazer cars had been built. The marque was phased out after a short run of face-lifted 1951 models.

The 1950 Frazers had themselves been leftovers, 1949 models that were used to fill a gap between the end of the '49 model year and '51. In K-F's case, '51 came early, in March of 1950. There was a four-door sedan in the standard series; a sedan and four-door convertible for the Manhattan line. The convertibles, hastily fabricated from sedan bodies and given heavy frames and body reinforcement, never sold well. Only 131 Frazer Manhattan convertibles were built in 1951. They sold for the price of a Cadillac, and buyers couldn't see paying that much for a K-F car. The convertibles were unique, however. They were the first postwar "convertible sedans," preceding the '61 Lincoln Continentals by more than a decade.

Frazers were powered by a 226 cubic-inch L-head "Supersonic" Six, which had been designed by Continental and built by Kaiser-Frazer. The power plant produced 112 hp in 1950 and 115 hp in 1951. Hydramatic transmission was a $159 option in 1951. Overdrive was available in both years for $96. The cars rode an especially long wheelbase for their class—123.5 inches. This made for good ride characteristics. They were economical and handled well. Luxury Manhattans were fitted with fine Bedford cord and nylon upholstery fabrics in colors harmonizing with the paint scheme, and full leather upholstery was available.

Model year 1951 was a cleanup year for Frazer. At the time, Kaiser cars were using a brand-new body, but the Frazers were merely restyled 1949-50 Kaisers. The restyling made the Frazers look radically different, however, and 50,000 orders were placed. Yet far fewer than that were built, and the marque came to an end as soon as all the old Kaiser bodies were used up.

Leftover Kaiser utility sedans, with rear hatches

1949-50 Manhattan sedan. Price: $2595.

1951 Manhattan four-door hardtop, $3075.

and folding rear seat, were converted into Frazer Vagabonds; former Kaiser Virginian four-door hardtops became Manhattan sedans; pillared sedans were assigned to the standard Frazer series but were trimmed similarly to the previous year's Manhattans. Altogether, 10,214 of the '51 Frazers were sold.

Kaiser-Frazer's styling department had created numerous renderings for future Frazers, based on the new 1951 Kaiser styling. However, with Joe Frazer out of the corporate picture in '51, the Kaisers decided to discontinue the Frazer and concentrate on their new small car, the Henry J.

FRAZER AT A GLANCE 1950-1959

Model Year	1950	1951	1952	1953	1954	1955	1956	1957	1958	1959
Price Range, $	2395-3295	2359-3075								
Weight Range, Lbs.	3386-3726	3456-3941								
Wheelbases, Ins.	123.5	123.5								
6 Cyl Engines, BHP	112	115								

Henry J

Kaiser-Frazer Corp., Willow Run, Michigan

Kaiser-Frazer was at the crossroads in 1949. The company had degenerated from healthy, record-high production in 1948 to just a skeleton the following year—dropping from eighth place in the industry to 16th. Henry Kaiser decided to press on. He borrowed $44 million from the Reconstruction Finance Corporation to maintain inventories and tool up for new models. This caused the abrupt departure of co-founder J.W. Frazer. Kaiser promised his lenders that part of the loan would go toward a small car that all Americans could afford to buy new. The Henry J was it.

Designer Howard "Dutch" Darrin had suggested a short-wheelbase compact related to his beautiful 1951 Kaiser, which was already locked up during Henry J planning. But Kaiser wanted something all-new. He settled on a prototype built by American

1951 Deluxe, priced at $1499.

1952 Corsair Deluxe. Price: $1552.

Metal Products, a Detroit supplier of frames and springs for car seats. Darrin reluctantly tried to make the ugly little two-door sedan look decent, applying his trademark "dip" in the beltline and little tailfins.

For power, K-F used Willys-built L-head Fours and Sixes of 134 and 161 cubic inches. The Four produced 68 bhp; the Six, 80. Incredible economy was promised for the Four, while the six-cylinder J turned out to be a hot-rod, giving 0 to 60 times in the 14-second range with its 2300-pound body. Though built on a 100-inch wheelbase, the Henry J could handle four passengers and a considerable amount of luggage. At a price of $1363, the basic four-cylinder car cost about $200 less than a Chevrolet.

K-F began its 1951 model year early, in March 1950. For a while, the J was in demand: nearly 82,000 of the '51 models were sold. Unfortunately, that saturated the market. Sales dropped quickly and dramatically by the end of 1952.

The 1952-54 models got a mild face lift—a restyled full-width grille, repositioned taillights and new interiors. An interim model marketed in an effort to use up the unwanted '51s was the 1952 Henry J Vagabond. It was merely a 1951 model with a "continental" outside spare tire. The price of the Vagabond was $1407 for the Four and $1552 for the Six.

By 1954, when the last 1123 reserialed 1953s were sold, it was evident that the Henry J project had collapsed. Many felt that the original approach had been wrong. The austere, stripped 1951 models—which lacked glove boxes, trunk lids, and other features normally held essential—were just too plain to be attractive. "I would have brought it out dressed up," said J.W. Frazer, "and undressed it later."

Advance plans for Henry J hardtops and convertibles were dropped. Total production for the four model years came to about 120,000.

HENRY J AT A GLANCE 1950-1959

Model Year	1950	1951	1952	1953	1954	1955	1956	1957	1958	1959
Price Range, $		1363-1499	1407-1664	1399-1561	1404-1566					
Weight Range, Lbs.		2293-2341	2365-2405	2395-2445	2405-2455					
Wheelbases, Ins.		100	100	100	100					
4 Cyl Engines, BHP		68	68	68	68					
6 Cyl Engines, BHP		80	80	80	80					

Hudson

Hudson Motor Car Co., Detroit, Michigan
Hudson Division of American Motors Corp., Kenosha, Wisconsin

The unit-body, "Step-down" Hudson introduced for 1948 had been a tremendous success for the old company, but it was a harbinger of disaster in the middle '50s.

The Step-down was hard to restyle—impossible, some designers said. By 1954, buyers were turned off by what they regarded as the same basic shape they'd first seen six years earlier. Also, Hudson offered only six-cylinder engines in '53 and '54. Though they were good engines, a Six was difficult to sell in the middle-priced field. Hudson's reaction to marketing opportunities was either too little or too late. Never did it produce a Step-down station wagon; never did it offer air conditioning. Roy D. Chapin Jr., who was a Hudson sales executive in the 1950s, explained the situation this way: "If you don't have enough money to do something and do it right, and if you haven't learned to specialize in a given thing. . .sooner or later you find you just can't do everything. [Hudson was] usually reacting, rather than anticipating."

Hudson entered the 1950s in fine fettle. It sold more than 143,000 cars in 1950, of which over 60,000 were new Pacemakers. Generally priced under $2000, Pacemakers used a destroked version of the flat-head Super Six engine. The 232 cubic-inch power plant produced 112 bhp at 4000 rpm. This performance was as good as that of the top-line Nash Ambassador, and put Pacemaker well ahead of the cars in its own price class.

Other '50 models were the Super Six and Super Eight; and the Commodore Six and Commodore Eight, ranging in price up to about $2900. The Six was a 262 cubic-inch unit producing 123 hp at 4000 rpm; the Eight actually had a smaller displacement, 254 cid, but yielded 128 hp at 4200 rpm.

All models were available with overdrive, and Drive-Master or Supermatic Drive, two Hudson semiautomatics of some repute. Drive-Master relieved the driver of the need to shift and declutch. The car was started by placing the shift lever in "high" and accelerating. The driver would ease up on the accelerator when the shift to regular drive was desired. With Supermatic, a high cruising gear was added. The shift to the high gear occurred automatically at 22 mph when the Supermatic dashboard button was engaged. In 1950, overdrive cost $95 extra; Drive-Master cost $105; Supermatic was priced at $199. None of them was a substitute for full automatic transmission, of course. When Hudson added proprietary Hydra-matic in 1951 at only $158 extra, Supermatic was dropped.

The Hudson Hornet, equipped with its powerful 308 cubic-inch Six, was introduced in 1951. It was

1951 Hornet Hollywood hardtop, $2869.

1953 Super Jet sedan, priced at $1954.

1953 Super Wasp sedan. Price: $2466.

available in four body styles, priced exactly the same as the Commodore Eight. The Hornet engine, with 3.8x4.5-inch bore and stroke, produced only 145 bhp at 3800 rpm in stock form, but was capable of much more than that in the hands of precision tuners. The most famous of these, Marshall Teague, claimed he could get 112 mph from a Hornet certified as stock by AAA or NASCAR. He was helped by an enthusiastic cadre of Hudson

Hudson

engineers, who introduced "severe usage" options that were in reality disguised racing modifications. Twin H-Power offered in 1953 consisted of twin carb and dual manifold induction, the first dual manifold on a Six, which greatly improved breathing. The "7-X" racing engine which arrived in late 1953 used .020 overbored cylinders, special cam and head, larger valves, higher compression, Twin H-Power and headers. The 7-X engines produced about 210 bhp.

The Hudson Hornet was invincible in AAA and NASCAR racing during most of 1951-54. Teague finished his 1952 AAA season with a 1000-point lead over his nearest rival. He'd won 12 of the 13 stock-car events. NASCAR drivers like Herb Thomas, Dick Rathmann, Al Keller and Frank Mundy drove Hornets to 27 victories in 1952, 21 in 1953 and 17 in 1954. Usually, three out of every four Hornets that entered a race would finish. Even in 1955, when the Step-down was replaced by a Nash-body car, 1954 Hornets still won a few races.

But the Hornet's racing successes weren't enough to keep the Hudson ship afloat. Though the company kept adding and subtracting model series through 1954, it was unable to add new body styles. The standard Pacemaker and the Super Eight were dropped for 1951, when the Hornet and the Hollywood hardtop were added; the Wasp replaced the Super Six for 1952. All the Commodores were discontinued for 1953, and the line of big cars was cut. A lower-priced Hornet Special in 1954 failed to spark sales. Throughout this period, Hudson could offer only two wheelbases and four basic body styles. Production dropped accordingly: from the 1950 high, Hudson built 93,000 for calendar 1951; 76,000 for 1952 and 1953; and only 32,000 for 1954.

The Step-down cried for total restyling by 1952, but Hudson couldn't afford it. The firm had sunk $12 million into a compact, the 105-inch-wheelbase Jet, in 1953. Using old Commodore Eight tooling, the Jet's 202 cubic-inch engine had a 3x4.8-inch bore and stroke. The Jet's Six produced 104 bhp. Twin H-power and a high-compression head were optional, and made for a speedy package. Jets were roadable and well built, but they weren't pretty. Over the objections of chief designer Frank Spring, management had insisted on bolt-upright, slab-sided styling that failed to impress many customers. Hudson tried hard, adding a very cheap Family Club sedan and luxurious Jet Liner models in 1954, but the cars did poorly.

The Jet did spark a project that might have become the long-awaited new Hudson: the Italia. This four-place grand turismo on a Jet chassis was designed by Spring and built by Carrozzeria Touring of Milan. Italias had wraparound windshields, doors cut into the roof, fender scoops that ducted cooling air to the brakes, flow-through ventilation, and form-fitting leather seats. Italias were built lower than production '54 Hornets by 10 inches. Though the Italias were powered by the 114-hp Hornet engine, they weren't very fast; the aluminum body was not very solid. But these were problems that might have been handled had Hudson had the money for a major commitment. There was no money. The firm's conservative engineers did not hold much hope for the wild, European body

1954 Hornet Special club sedan, $2571.

1954 Italia, priced at $4800.

1955 Hornet Hollywood hardtop, $3145.

anyway. Only 25 "production" Italias, plus the prototype and a four-door derivative called X-161, were built. Chapin served as Italia sales manager, and shoved them out as fast as he could at $4800 a copy. "I got rid of them." he said, adding, "It wasn't one of my greatest accomplishments."

Late in 1953, rumors began circulating of a Hudson-Nash merger. Nash couldn't have come calling at a better time. Hudson sales were sinking: the books were written in red ink. Between January 1, 1954, and the end of April that year when Hudson closed as an independent company, it had already lost over $6 million on sales of only $28.7 million. Old-hat styling, the Jet, a weak dealer network and insufficient capital for expansion were the reasons.

In merger talks, George Mason of Nash insisted on one big condition: the Jet had to go. Hudson President A.E. Barit fought this, but not for long. He was in a very poor position to bargain.

The merger was really a Nash takeover. Hudson's Detroit plant was soon closed and all production was transferred to Kenosha, Wisconsin. And everybody recognized the all-new 1955 Hudson: it was a Nash. The car featured Nash's unit-construction sedan and hardtop bodies, with a special egg-crate grille, distinct trim and rear end. A reference to previous Hudsons was the '55 Hudson's dashboard, which used the old 1954 instruments. Wasps were powered by the former Jet 202 cubic-inch engine; the 308 Six was retained for the Hornet; the Hornet V8 used a 320 Packard mill of 208 bhp. Twin H-Power was available on the Sixes, increasing the Wasp's horsepower from 110 to 120 and the Hornet's from 160 to 170.

Wasp's wheelbase was 114.3 inches; Hornet's was 121.3. Top of the line was the Hornet V8 Custom Hollywood hardtop at $3145. A badge-engineered line of Metropolitans and Ramblers also was offered by Nash.

American Motors introduced its own 190-hp V8 for 1956, replacing the Packard unit in midseason as the Hornet "Special." The small Wasp Six remained, as did the Hornet Six, along with the usual assortment of so-called Hudson Ramblers. "V-line Styling" was the way AMC described the horrendous chrome-plated nightmare allegedly

1956 Hornet Custom sedan, $3026.

1957 Hornet Custom Hollywood hardtop, $3101.

created by Edmund E. Anderson. It was the ugliest Hudson in a generation; and it was equipped with the AMC V8, far less powerful than the Packard unit. The new power plant together with the terrible styling made for depressing sales. Only 10,671 non-Rambler Hudsons were peddled in 1956. In the next year—Hudson's last—styling didn't improve, and only 3,876 big Hudsons were sold. They were all V8 models. Rambler was listed as a separate make, but a rumor that Ramblers would diverge into very different Hudson and Nash models came to naught. There was no money for that.

The AMC decision to drop Hudson and Nash, Chapin said, was only common sense. "We ran Hudson and Nash Metropolitans and Ramblers—it was a charade. They were basically the exact same automobiles, and the decision really was one that said we've got to spend our money and our effort and our concentration on the Rambler because we haven't got the dough to update the big Nashes and the big Hudsons."

HUDSON AT A GLANCE 1950-1959

Model Year	1950	1951	1952	1953	1954	1955	1956	1957	1958	1959
Price Range, $	1806-2893-	1964-3099	2116-3342	1858-3342	1621-4800	1445-4800	1672-3159	2821-3101		
Weight Range, Lbs.	3445-3865	3380-3800	3305-3770	2650-3760	2635-3800	1803-3878	2891-3926	3631-3693		
Wheelbases, Ins.	119, 124	119, 124	119, 124	105-124	105-124	108-121.3	108-121.3	121.3		
6 Cyl Engines, BHP	112, 123	112-145	112-145	104-145	104-160	90-170	120, 170			
8 Cyl Engines, BHP	128	128	128			208	190, 208	255		

Imperial
Chrysler and Imperial Division of Chrysler Corp., Detroit, Michigan

Imperial became a separate and distinct make in 1955, and remained as such through 1975. Prior to that, it had long been a Chrysler model. Imperial couldn't shake its image as a Chrysler, but it had some of its most successful years in the 1950s.

The beautiful 1955-56 models, based extensively on Virgil Exner's custom Parade Phaetons and the Chrysler K-310 sports car, are recognized by many collectors today as the most desirable Imperials of all. Wearing a distinctive split grille up front and "bombsite" taillights, elegantly trimmed inside and out, these big sedans and hardtops still look very good today. The '55s were powered by a 331 cubic-inch V8, a hemi-head of 250 horsepower; the '56 models were powered by a bored-out version of the same engine—354 cubic inches, 280 hp. The 1956s rode a wheelbase of 133 inches instead of 130, which made them the longest Imperials. Wheelbase shrank to 129 inches in 1957. The 1956 models were given tailfins, and no other Chrysler product of the day wore its fins as well. The styling was nicely integrated, and almost appeared to have been designed from the ground up, rather than the quick face lift it was. The only significant optional

1955 Imperial hardtop, $4720.

1956 Imperial sedan, $4832.

extra for 1955-56 Imperials was air conditioning, priced at $567. The cars were comprehensively equipped, with PowerFlite transmission standard. Though not in the class of Chrysler's 300, the Imperials were lively performers. Yet they were surprisingly economical: Imperials won luxury-class laurels in the Mobilgas Economy Runs.

Crown Imperial formal cars were available as sedans or limousines in 1955-56. Built in Detroit on the 149.5-inch limo wheelbase, they replaced all previous Dodge, De Soto and Chrysler long-wheelbase cars. Nicely styled along the lines of the standard Imperial, they sold by the dozen. A total of 398 were produced for both model years; 96 of them were eight-passenger sedans and the rest were limousines. New for 1956 was a four-door hardtop, the Southampton, priced at $5225.

For 1957 came all-new Exner Forward Look styling. Imperials sprouted huge tailfins and a full-width, complicated-looking grille. In an effort to surpass Lincoln, which was then selling in second place behind Cadillac in the luxury field, Chrysler added two new series, the Imperial Crown and LeBaron. More luxuriously trimmed than standard cars, the Crown came as a sedan, two- and four-door hardtops, and a new convertible which was the first soft-top Imperial model that had been offered since 1953. The LeBaron series, added in January 1957, comprised a pillar sedan and four-door Southampton hardtop. Both new series were priced about $600 higher than the basic Imperial model. All '57s came with TorqueFlite three-speed automatic transmission, and a 392 hemi that produced 325 horsepower.

From 1957 through 1965, Crown Imperial limousines were built by Ghia of Turin, Italy. Based on potential sales, Chrysler could no longer justify the time and space necessary to build them in Detroit. Against a potential $3.3 million tooling bill at home, Ghia offered to tool Crown Imperials for only $15,000, provided Chrysler could ship the basic "kit" to Turino. Each Ghia limousine began as an unfinished two-door Imperial hardtop on a rigid convertible chassis, shipped to Italy with all body panels intact. Ghia cut the car apart. added 20.5 inches to the wheelbase, reworked the structure above the beltline, fitted and trimmed the luxurious interior, and finished off the bodies using 150 pounds of lead. Each car required a month to be built, and initial delays made the Crown Imperial a very late introduction in 1957. Priced at a stratospheric $15,075, the car's sales were not impressive: only 36 were sold in 1957, only 31 in '58, and just seven in '59. Only 132 Ghia Crowns had been built by the time the line ended in 1965, but all of them

1957 Crown convertible, $5598.

1958 Crown Southampton, $5632.

1957 Crown Imperial limousine by Ghia, $15,075.

1959 Crown convertible. Price: $5774.

were impeccably tailored, all-out luxury machines.

Imperial's best year ever was 1957. By building nearly 38,000 cars for the calendar year, Imperial just edged out Lincoln for the only time in history The 1958s were therefore changed only slightly. Circular parking lights and a complex mesh and egg-crate grille are the quickest ways to distinguish them. The same basic lineup was offered, and prices were only marginally higher. Horsepower, however, was boosted again, to 345 (Crown Imperials continued to use the 325-hp engine). The year proved to be a poor one for Chrysler products in general; Imperial dropped back behind Lincoln, and produced only 13,673 cars for the 12 months. Though production reached about 20,000 in 1959, it never rose higher than that. To the frustration of dealers, people still called the cars "Chrysler Imperials"—and a "Chrysler," though prestigious, didn't have the charisma of a Cadillac.

Imperials for 1959 used the basic 1957 bodies, combined with a toothy grille and added brightwork along the sides. For the first time the standard series received a model designation, Custom. The lineup of bodies and styles was unchanged. Offered again were Torsion-Aire front suspension, TorqueFlite automatic and "Full-Time" power steering. In the engine department, however, Imperial switched to the 413 cubic-inch wedge-head V8 which produced 350 hp at 4600 rpm. It provided performance comparable to that of the hemi, but was more economical to build and maintain.

Aside from the Ghia Crowns, the rarest and most desirable Imperials of the '50s are the glamorous convertibles. Production figures by model year are: 1167 for 1957; 675 for 1958; and 555 for 1959. Production was evenly divided between standard Imperials and Imperial Crowns; the LeBaron sedans accounted for only a few thousand each year.

IMPERIAL AT A GLANCE 1950-1959

Model Year	1950	1951	1952	1953	1954	1955	1956	1957	1958	1959
Price Range, $						4483-7095	4832-7731	4736-15,075	4839-15,075	4910-15,075
Weight Range, Lbs.						4490-5230	4555-5205	4640-5960	4590-5960	4675-5960
Wheelbases, Ins.						130, 149.5	133, 149.5	129, 149.5	129, 149.5	129, 149.5
8 Cyl Engines, BHP						250	280	325	325, 345	325, 350

Kaiser

Kaiser-Frazer Corp., Willow Run, Michigan
Kaiser Motors Corp., Toledo, Ohio

Though a handful of 1950 model Kaisers were sold (sedans, Travelers, Virginian hardtops and four-door convertibles), the real focus for the '50s was on the new "Anatomic" 1951 Kaiser. The slender, beautiful car designed by Howard "Dutch" Darrin was supposed to have been ready for 1950. However, a glut of 1949 models forced Kaiser to give the leftover '49s 1950 serial numbers and

1949-50 Virginian, priced at $2995.

1951 Deluxe sedan, priced at $2328.

1952 Virginian Deluxe club coupe. Price: $2296.

shove them out the door until the stock was used up.

By early 1950, the new Kaiser was in production. The car's public debut was set for March of that year, six months ahead of normal introduction time. Kaiser sales rocketed upward. Close to 140,000 of the 1951 models were sold, against about 15,000 of the 1950s. From a dismal 16th place in the industry in 1949, Kaiser-Frazer shot up to 12th. A total of 146,911 cars were built for calendar 1950; nearly 100,000 for 1951.

There was reason to be enthusiastic about the '51 Kaiser. From every angle it was unlike any other American car of its day. It offered 700 square inches more glass area than its nearest competitor, and a beltline lower than that of any Detroit car produced through 1956. The unique styling was complemented by an array of bright exterior colors and exciting interiors—the work of Carleton Spencer.

Kaiser was probably the first company to really push safety. For 1951 it advertised the padded dash, recessed instruments, narrow windshield corner posts, outstanding visibility, and a windshield that popped out onto the hood if struck with a force of more than 35 pounds per square inch. The engineering, too, was commendable. Engineers John Widman and Ralph Isbrandt shunned unit-body construction, but built a very rigid separate body and chassis on a frame that weighed only 200 pounds. A low center of gravity gave Kaiser surprisingly good handling. A Chrysler engineer who sampled one commented, "It rides like one of our 4500-pound cars." Yet the Kaiser weighed only about 3100 pounds. The engine was not new, but was held over from previous models. The 226 cubic-inch L-head Six developed 115 hp. Many felt that a V8 would have made the car unbeatable, and the lack of one hurt Kaiser sales as the '50s wore on.

The face-lifted '52s weren't quite ready by the end of 1951; in the interim, K-F offered the 1952 Kaiser Virginian. K-F built about 6000 of these, which were nearly identical to the 1951 line and comprised the same body styles: sedans, club coupes, business coupes, and the Traveler utility cars. A Traveler looked like a normal sedan when buttoned up, but a hatch was built into the rear of the body; it opened to reveal a huge cargo compartment. The Traveler rear seat folded too, like a station wagon's.

The same group of models was offered for the rest of 1952. Their most significant styling changes from the year before were "teardrop" taillights and a heavier-looking grille. Kaiser now called the top series Manhattan (an old Frazer model name) and

1953 Deluxe Traveler. Price: $2619.

1953 "Hardtop" Dragon, priced at $3924.

the lowest series Deluxe instead of Special. The later '52s are fairly rare: only 7500 Deluxes and 19,000 Manhattans were built in the short model year before they were superceded by the 1953s.

The 1953 Kaiser Hardtop Dragon sedan was the most luxurious of the marque, priced at $3924. It was inspired by Spencer's Dragon trim option on 1951 models, but appeared for 1953 as a series in its own right. Distinguished by gold-plated exterior trim—hood ornament, badges, script and trunk keyhole cover—the Dragon also featured a padded top, usually made of "bambu" vinyl. This tough, oriental-style material also covered the dash and parts of the seats and door panels. Cloth sections of the seats were done in "Laguna" cloth, a fabric with an oblong pattern created by fashion designer Marie Nichols. The Dragon came standard with every possible option: tinted glass, Hydra-matic drive, whitewalls, dual-speaker radio, and Calpoint custom carpeting on the floor and in the trunk. A gold medallion on the dash was engraved with the owner's name. The Dragon was a spectacular car, but its price restricted sales. Only 1277 Dragons

were built altogether, and the last few were almost given away.

Aside from the Dragon, changes for 1953 were slight. Kaiser offered a stripped Carolina model starting at $2313, but sold only 1812 of them. The company admitted that the Carolina's chief purpose was to draw people into the showrooms. The two-door Travelers were eliminated, along with the club coupes. Engines got a boost in horsepower to 118, and power steering was offered late in the season as a $122 option.

Kaiser sales were plummeting in these years. K-F built only 70,000 cars for calendar 1952 and only 22,000 (including Henry Js) for 1953. The Toledo-built '54 models were a last-ditch effort. They were cleverly face-lifted by stylist Buzz Grisinger. Their front ends were based on the Buick XP-300 show car, one of Edgar Kaiser's favorite designs. Their wide, concave grilles featured "floating" headlights. Rear styling was set off by Safety-Glo taillights—big, rounded affairs with a lighted strip running up along the top of the fenders.

In an effort to wring more power out of the 226

Prototype Darrin with split windshield, low fenders.

1954 Darrin, priced at $3668.

Kaiser

engine, a McCulloch centrifugal supercharger was bolted to Manhattans. It could produce 140 bhp, going into operation only when the accelerator was pressed to the floor. Alongside the two- and four-door Manhattans, K-F sold the unsupercharged Special in two models. The first batch was a group of warmed-over 1953 Manhattans with 1954 front ends—another effort to use up leftovers. The second was a genuine 1954 type, with wrap-around rear window like the '54 Manhattan's. Neither version did well. After about 8500 of the 1954s and 1291 of the 1955s (Manhattans only, with new serial numbers) were built, the dies were packed up and sent to a Kaiser affiliate in Argentina. In a tribute to the timelessness of its design, the car was produced there as the Kaiser Carabela through 1962.

Another memorable but unsuccessful experiment was the Kaiser Darrin sliding-door sports car of 1954, based on the 100-inch-wheelbase Henry J chassis. Dutch Darrin designed it on his own in late 1952 and talked Henry Kaiser into marketing it for $3668. Its light fiberglass body and 90-hp Willys F-head Six gave the car adequate pickup, but the Darrin didn't go far. Only 435 were built as the company wound down.

The Darrin was beautifully styled, and is a prized collector's item today. In addition to unique sliding doors, it featured a landau top. This had an intermediate half-up position, held in place by a set of working landau irons. The car was equipped with full instrumentation and was usually fitted with a three-speed floor shift and overdrive. It delivered economy in the 30-mpg range, could do 0-60 in about 13 seconds, and could approach 100 mph top speed. Those were good figures for 1954. But the project was a big disappointment to Darrin. At the last minute, he bought about 100 leftovers from the factory, fitted some of them with Cadillac V8 engines, and sold them for $4350 each at his Los Angeles showroom. The Cadillac-powered Darrins

1954 Manhattan sedan. Price: $2670.

1955 Manhattan sedan. Price: $2670.

were potent indeed, capable of a top speed of about 140 mph.

The Kaiser automobile came to an end in America in 1955, after 10 years and a loss of $100 million. The cars were usually good ones, offering many innovative features, but they never seemed to make it with the American public. As Edgar Kaiser liked to say, the cars suffered not from poor quality, but from an identity crisis. "Slap a Buick nameplate on it," he remarked sadly, "and it would sell like hotcakes."

KAISER AT A GLANCE 1950-1959

Model Year	1950	1951	1952	1953	1954	1955	1956	1957	1958	1959
Price Range, $	1995-2288	1992-2433	1992-2759	2313-3924	2334-3668	2617-2670				
Weight Range, Lbs.	3311-3726	3106-3345	3110-3310	3135-3435	2175-3375	3335-3375				
Wheelbases, Ins.	123.5	118.5	118.5	118.5	100, 118.5	118.5				
6 Cyl Engines, BHP	100-112	115	115	118	90-140	140				

Lincoln

Lincoln-Mercury Division of Ford Motor Co., Dearborn, Michigan

For Lincoln, the '50s was a topsy-turvy decade. As they drove out of the 1940s, Lincolns were luxurious, but bulky and slow. By 1952, they'd been transformed into taut, powerful road cars; and they reigned supreme in the top American stock class at the Carrera Panamericana road race in Mexico. The Lincoln was overhauled again in 1956, and was dramatically changed into a very long, good-looking highway tourer. From 1957 on it grew fins, acquired some lamentable styling features and adopted the biggest engine in the business.

The 1950-51 Lincolns were of the school of bulbous styling—a look that emerged before and during WW II in Bob Gregorie's design offices at Ford. Easily distinguishable by their sunken headlamps (covered lights were intended first), they appear to be big Mercurys. The Lincoln model rode on a 121-inch wheelbase; the Cosmopolitan wheelbase was 125 inches. The Cosmopolitan shared no body panels with the concurrent Mercury, though the smaller Lincoln used Mercury panels from the cowl back. The explanation lies in Ford's postwar planning. Originally, the 118-inch-wheelbase Mercury was to have been the '49 Ford, and the 121-inch-wheelbase Lincoln was to have been the '49 Mercury. What became the Cosmopolitan was in fact the proposed '49 Zephyr—a model that never made it into production. (Neither did a new 1949 Continental, though many designs were considered.)

When Ford's policy committee, led by Ernest Breech and Harold Youngren, urged the adoption of a shorter, 114-inch wheelbase Ford, the proposed '49 designs were all moved up a notch and the Zephyr was eliminated. The ex-Mercury Lincoln was thus a much cheaper car than the Cosmopolitan. The latter had heavy chrome moldings over the front wheelwells and a more complicated grille than the Lincoln. Both cars, however, used the same engine—a 336.7 cubic-inch L-head originally designed for Ford trucks, producing 152 hp at 3600 rpm. From 1950 to 1954, Lincolns offered Hydra-matic transmission (optional 1950-51) that it bought from archrival General Motors. While not known for speed, this equipment was good enough for ninth place in the 1950 Mexican race. Also, a high-geared 1951 Lincoln actually won the Mobilgas economy run in '51 with a 25.5-mpg average.

The 1950 models featured a brand-new dashboard created by Tom Hibbard, who was then chief designer. The dash, an attractive, rolled affair with an oblong window covering the instruments, was popular enough to still be around as late as 1956.

1950 Sport Sedan, priced at $2574.

1950 Cosmopolitan for President Truman with retractable running boards.

1951 Sport Sedan, priced at $2796.

Longer rear fenders were adapted, and upright taillights replaced the round 1949-50 units in 1951. The grille was simplified, the wheel covers were changed, and horsepower was increased to 154. In 1950 and 1951, special limited editions were offered, with custom interiors and padded canvas tops. The Lincoln base series had the Lido, priced at $2720 and $2957; Cosmopolitans offered the

Lincoln

Capri, at $3405 and $3653. Not many were sold in this guise. As one of the completely restyled 1952 models, however, the Capri became a top series, while the heretofore ultraluxurious Cosmopolitan became the least expensive Lincoln.

Lincoln never did well with its bathtub-shaped 1949-51 cars: production during those years never rose higher than 1948's 44,000. Sales were generally a shade higher for 1952-54, but remained miles behind Cadillac. Perhaps this was a result of Lincoln's remarkable uniformity: the same five models were offered in all three years. Cosmopolitan and Capri were both available as four-door sedans and two-door hardtops; Capri also was offered as a convertible. Styling was on the sedate side, which may have been another problem. In retrospect, nevertheless, these were three of Lincoln's best years.

The most important mechanical feature of the 1952-54 models was Lincoln's new valve-in-head V8: 317.5 cubic inches, with a bore and stroke of 3.8x3.5 inches. It developed 160 hp in 1952 and 205 hp in 1953-54. It was a superior engine in many ways. The crankshaft, for example, had eight counterweights, rather than the six of its competitors. The intake valves were oversize, allowing better breathing, greater efficiency and more output for every cubic inch. (In 1953, Lincoln produced 0.64 hp per cubic inch, against 0.63 for Cadillac and 0.54 for the Chrysler hemi.) There was also a deep-skirt crankcase; the side of the case extended below the crankshaft centerline to create an extremely stiff support for the shaft.

There was more to the story than the engine. The 1952 Lincolns introduced the first ball-joint front suspension. This very flexible, controllable system was a precursor of the suspensions used by most cars today. Recirculating-ball power steering, oversize drum brakes, an optional four-way power seat and liberal sound-deadening insulation also were incorporated into the cars. Models equipped with optional factory air conditioning offered flow-through ventilation when the compressor was turned off. Fabrics and leathers, fit and finish were of a quality that far exceeded that of conventional Ford products.

Despite its short 123-inch wheelbase, the Lincoln of this period offered more room inside than preceding models did, and sometimes more than its successors would. Its visibility was better than that of any contemporary car except the Kaiser, and exterior trim was notably free of the era's excesses. The 1952-54 taillights, incidentally, deserve notice. They were fluted, like those of today's Mercedes-Benz. This design enabled them to shed water and dirt. Whether this was pure engineering

1952 Cosmopolitan sedan, $3517.

1953 Capri sedan. Price: $3766.

or just a lucky styling idea, the design functioned extremely well and the lights were good looking.

But all these good features are overshadowed by the Lincoln's performance in Mexico. In the second, third and fourth Carrera Panamericana, the cars had no rival in the International Standard Class. Lincolns took the top five places in 1952, the top four in 1953, and first and second in 1954. Major credit for the race preparation goes to Clay Smith, a gifted mechanic who was tragically killed in a pit accident in 1954. Smith had help from publicity-conscious Ford, which supplied him with "export" suspension, Ford truck camshafts, mechanical valve lifters, special front wheel spindles and hubs, and a choice of two optional rear ends. The higher axle enabled a Lincoln with a stock engine to top 130 mph. The 1952 race winner, Chuck Stevenson, actually finished the 2000-mile grind from Juarez to the Guatemala border nearly an hour ahead of the Ferrari that had won the year before.

Lincoln wasn't ready for a total redesign in 1955, and its line that year was the most conservative in the business. The wraparound windshield design was being used by almost every maker; but the

1953 Lincoln, Mexican Road Race champ.

1955 Capri hardtop, priced at $3910.

1954 Capri hardtop. Price: $3869.

1956 Premiere four-door sedan. Price: $4601.

Lincoln windshield was steadfastly traditional, and as a result, was more practical. The wheelbase remained at 123 inches, but weight increased by 50 to 100 pounds. The company finally offered its own automatic transmission, Turbo-Drive. Instead of Cosmopolitans, the bottom-line cars were called Customs; the Capri remained and the same five models were fielded. Styling was crisp, clean and timeless. Interiors were a luxurious combination of quality fabrics and top-grain leather. Sales, appropriately, were up for '55: once again, Lincoln sold more than 40,000 units for the calendar year.

A year of drastic change was 1956. "Unmistakably Lincoln," read the ads—but buyers had to look twice to see vestiges of the '56 in the newer edition. Gone were the short wheelbase and squarish styling. They were replaced by a 126-inch wheelbase chassis, and a body that was seven inches longer and three inches wider. Capri became the lower series; the ultimate Lincoln was called Premiere and was priced at up to $900 more than comparable top-line Lincolns of the year before. To give credit where due, the '56 Lincoln managed this new, enlarged body extremely well. The grille was clean, with peaked headlights and

simple ornamentation; two-toning was confined to the roof; at the rear end were rakish vertical taillights capping long exhaust ports and a "grille" motif duplicating the front design. The engine was as new as the styling. The 368 cubic-inch V8 produced 285 bph at 4600 rpm—"True power," the ads said, "that works for your safety at every speed." Despite their bulk, the cars didn't weigh much more than the 1955 models. As the only company with a restyle for 1956 instead of a mere face lift, Lincoln did well. Almost 50,000 cars were built for the 12 months. This was still only about a third of Cadillac's total, but was encouraging to Lincoln nevertheless. Lincoln made plans for a radical face lift in 1957.

Among the changes for '57 was the first different Lincoln body style offered since 1951. This four-door hardtop, dubbed the Landau, was Lincoln's response to a popular Detroit trend toward that design. Landaus were offered in both the Capri ($4794) and Premiere ($5294) lines. The Premiere convertible, priced at $5381, was still the most expensive Lincoln. Pointy tailfins sprouted, and four-lamp front end styling was adopted a bit in advance of most competitors. With 10:1 com-

Lincoln

pression, the 368 V8 engine delivered up to 300 horsepower. Lincoln had a good year in '57, but not a great one. It sold slightly fewer cars than Imperial (for the only time in history) and pinned its hopes for '58 on yet another total restyling.

Model year 1958 proved to be a very bad one for an investment of millions of dollars into new tooling. The economy bottomed out, and car sales dropped by 50 percent or more from 1957 levels. Elsewhere at Ford, the Edsel was beginning its rapid slide to nowhere, Mercury sales were running 40 percent behind 1957 and Ford was trailing Chevrolet by a quarter million units. The new Lincolns were longer, lower and wider at a time when even some luxury-car buyers were thinking in terms of compact dimensions. Calendar-year production accordingly dropped to about 26,000. The Premier, which had carried the bulk of Lincoln sales since 1956, barely sold 10,000 units for the

1957 Premiere 4-door sedan, priced at $5294.

1958 Premiere hardtop, priced at $5318.

model year. All told, little more than 17,000 of the 1958 models were sold.

At the bottom of this avalanche stood the 1958 Lincoln, longer by six inches than 1957, with a 131-inch wheelbase. It was easily recognized, for there wasn't much else like it: sharp tailfins; pointed front fenders carrying four headlights in slanted recesses; a heavily chromed grille; and gigantic flared bumpers. Under the hood was the largest engine used in an American passenger car for 1958—the 430 cubic-inch Continental V8 of 375 horsepower. An argument could be made that the Lincoln formula was nevertheless right. Recession or no, buyers in this class were still demanding cars of the Lincoln's type. Yet Cadillac was attracting more people with a less radical face lift, and Imperial was garnering residual sales with its finned wonders. The two rivals had recently expanded with many new series and body styles, and Cadillac's comparable models were priced several hundred dollars lower than Lincoln's. It was the 1958 debacle that ushered in Elwood Engel and the three-year styling program that culminated in the all-new, razor-edged Lincolns of 1961.

In the meantime, Lincoln returned for 1959 with the only thing it had: more of the same. The Premiere convertible had been eliminated in 1958, and the '59 lineup was identical to that year's—four-door sedan, and two- and four-door hardtop in Capri and Premiere series. Up ahead of Lincoln in price was the Continental, still a make on its own and available in a wide variety of body styles. Lincoln sales had reached near-crisis levels. Only about 7800 each of Capri and Premiere were sold.

Mechanically, the cars were basic 1958s, but horsepower was decreased again to 350. In desperation, Lincoln held prices to about where they'd been in 1958. The company would still have to struggle through 1960 before relief came in the form of Engel's new models. It was a sad end to a decade that had begun with so much promise.

Today, collector interest runs parallel to buyer interest of 20 years ago. The most collectible '50s Lincolns (considering Continental as a separate make) are the "Road Race" 1952-54 cars; some interest is stirring in 1950-51 bathtubs and the 1956-57 models; and the market is virtually inactive for the 1958-59 models.

LINCOLN AT A GLANCE 1950-1959

Model Year	1950	1951	1952	1953	1954	1955	1956	1957	1958	1959
Price Range, $	2527-3948	2745-4234	3517-4025	3522-4031	3522-4031	3563-4072	4119-4747	4649-5381	4951-5565	4902-5594
Weight Range, Lbs.	3970-4490	4065-4615	4140-4350	4125-4350	4135-4310	4185-4415	4305-4452	4373-4676	4735-4880	4741-4887
Wheelbases, Ins.	121, 125	121, 125	123	123	123	123	126	126	131	131
8 Cyl Engines, BHP	152	154	160	205	205	225	285	300	375	350

Mercury

Lincoln-Mercury Division of Ford Motor Co.,
Dearborn, Michigan

Immediately upon its introduction in 1939, Mercury attracted a large following of people who liked the idea of a car offering more power and prestige than a Ford. During the '50s, Mercury occupied sixth to eighth place in the production race, usually building between 150,000 and 250,000 cars a year. Positioned in the market midway between Ford and Lincoln, the Mercury sometimes tended to be ignored by corporate officials; it often got its styling and engineering features from the other two makes as hand-me-downs. By the close of the 1950s, however, Mercury's importance in the Ford scheme was well established. After the failure of the Edsel, a broad line of Mercurys priced in the lower-medium class was essential.

The 1949-51 Mercury was an excellent value, considering that it was styled similarly to the Lincoln but sold at a lower price. Power came from a 255.4 cubic-inch L-head V8, which was about 12 percent larger than Ford's and offered 15 more horsepower. Many felt this made up for the extra 300-some pounds a Mercury carried. The cars became a hot-rodder's favorite, second only to Ford itself in the early '50s.

Essentially, the 1950-51 Mercury line consisted of only one model; it was available as a two- or four-door sedan, two-door semi-wood wagon, and a convertible. Also available was the Monterey, a low-production sport coupe with special trim and a padded top of either canvas or leather. Mercury was very late to get a hardtop, and Monterey filled the gap in the meantime.

It isn't easy to tell the '50s and '51s apart at a glance. The 1951 has a semicircular crest and Mercury name above the grille, while the '50 spells the name out on a hood chrome strip and uses a smaller crest. Parking light housings are larger on the '51 than on the '50, sweeping back to the front wheel wells. The 1951 models use a different rear fender treatment—more upright, with rounded corners dropping straight down to the rear bumper. Mercury's V8 developed 110 hp in 1950, 112 in 1951. And 1951 was the first year for Merc-O-Matic, the two-speed automatic developed in cooperation with the Warner Gear Division of Borg-Warner.

Mercury ran seventh in production in 1950 with 334,000 units; then eighth in 1951 with 239,000. Ford Motor Company was the only maker to introduce a completely new restyling for 1952, and Mercury received the same tight, clean styling that was applied to Lincoln. Its wheelbase was unchanged. The L-head V8 was retained, but its power was boosted to 125 hp by means of a higher compression ratio.

1950 Monterey special coupe, $2150.

1951 Sport Sedan. The price: $2189.

1952 Custom hardtop, which sold for $2313.

Model year 1952 was a time for model shuffling, and Mercury appeared in two series. The Custom offered two- and four-door sedans; a four-door, all-steel station wagon available in six- and eight-passenger models; and the new Mercury hardtop. The Monterey line, becoming a separate

Mercury

line, included a convertible, hardtop and sedan. Montereys were luxuriously upholstered in quality broadcloth for sedans, and leather and vinyl for the hardtop and the convertible. Single colors were available on the sedan, but the hardtop came with two-tone paint as standard equipment. The Mercury dashboard was an interesting innovation. Aircraft-type toggle levers flanked the central gauge cluster and controlled the heating and ventilation system. Mercury sales fell along with those of the rest of the industry in 1952, partly because of Korean War restrictions on production. Yet the restyled line accounted for 172,087 units, and calendar year production of 195,000 units was good enough to put Mercury in eighth place. Business picked up in 1953 and Mercury built over 320,000 cars—rising to sixth position, its highest ever.

The Mercury line remained the same for 1953, except for the shifting of the four-door station wagon from the Custom to the Monterey series, and the discontinuation of the six-passenger version. Prices went up by only a few dollars. Though its engine was quickly becoming obsolete, the Mercury offered good value in these years—high performance and acceptable economy. Only minor styling changes were made, with the grille receiving heavy bullet-type bumper guards, for example. A four-way power seat and power brakes were offered as optional equipment.

A significant engineering change came in 1954, when Mercury joined Ford in a switch to overhead-valve V8 engines. Mercury's V8 displaced more cubic inches than the Ford power plant. At 256 cubic inches, it was the same size as the previous L-head, but of squarer bore and stroke (3.62x3.10). It developed 161 horsepower at 4400 rpm. With a low 3.9:1 rear axle ratio and standard transmission, it was fast off the line. The Mercury engine used a five-main-bearing crankshaft and came in standard form with a four-barrel carburetor. Another major mechanical change was the use of ball-joint suspension on the Mercury front end. Styling was also measurably improved by the addition of wraparound taillights and a clean grille. The model lineup stayed the same, with the addition of a new model that is perhaps more famous among collectors today than it was in 1954: the Monterey Sun Valley.

Ford's styling department had for some time experimented with plastic-topped cars: Sun Valley (and the comparable Ford Skyliner) was the result. In theory it was fine, a sort of cross between the airy feeling of a convertible and the comfort of a closed hardtop. In practice, it was something else. Though the plastic half of the roof was tinted and a shade was provided for really hot weather, drivers still complained that it was like an oven inside, and

sales weren't impressive. But the '54 Sun Valley was the most attractive of this short-lived Ford breed. It came in select color combinations of yellow, or mint green and a dark green top. Embellished with gold-anodized fender script, it was a handsome automobile. The price of $2582—some $130 above the standard hardtop—was forbidding. Mercury was most successful with the 1954 Sun Valley, of which 9761 were sold. The 1955 version, second and last, sold only 1787 copies.

At 256,000 sales, 1954 wasn't the greatest year Mercury had ever had, but high hopes were truly realized in 1955. With all new styling, a new V8 and the first wheelbase increase since 1942, the '55s couldn't miss. Over 434,000 sales were run up for a record that still stands. These were the most appealing Mercurys in years, offered in more models

1953 Mercury Monterey four-door sedan, $2333.

1954 Monterey Sun Valley, $2582.

and series than ever before.

Line leader for '55 was the brand-new Montclair, offered as a four-door sedan, hardtop, convertible and Sun Valley at prices ranging from $2631 to $2712. It was nicely styled, used an evolutionary form of the 1954 grille, and was distinguished by a thin color panel outlined in bright metal under the side windows. Next came the Monterey sedan, hardtop and wagon, followed by the '55 Custom series in the same body styles plus a two-door sedan. The engine was a 292 cubic-inch V8 developing 188 hp; in the Montclair, or optionally on other models, it produced 198 hp with an 8.5:1 compression ratio, and came only with Merc-O-Matic transmission.

In 1956, Ed Sullivan announced "The Big M" line, yet another ambitious expansion into somewhat uncharted territory. Mercury prices were on the rise, and to keep the product competitive the cut-rate Medalist was aimed at the bottom-line buyer. There were four Medalists: two- and four-door hardtops, and two- and four-door sedans. Unfortunately, inflation took its toll. The "low-priced" Medalists were actually more expensive than the previous year's Mercury Customs. At the same time, they weren't priced far enough below the better-trimmed 1956 Customs. Although Lincoln-Mercury dealers pushed hard with the price-leading Medalist two-door sedan, a total of only 45,812 Medalist models were sold. Customs, Montereys and Montclairs all surpassed the Medalist by at least double its production. The car was accordingly dropped for 1957. Curiously, it reappeared in 1958 before finally passing out of the picture. The face-lift year of 1956 brought about changes that were useful updates of the 1955 restyling. Side molding was connected front-to-back in a sort of lightning-bolt motif that was attractive and new looking. Four-door hardtops had arrived in force, in all four Mercury ranges. They were known as Phaetons, and they sold well—even outselling the standard four-door sedan in the Montclair series. Throughout the line Mercurys used an enlarged 312 cubic-inch V8 that provided 210 horsepower in standard form and up to 235 hp on the Monterey and Montclair. But it was a downbeat year for auto companies. Mercury was no exception. Only about 247,000 cars rolled off the Mercury assembly lines in those 12 months, far below the 1955 pace. A most promising series was the Montclair, however, which managed to sell almost as many units in 1956 as it had in 1955. This was an achievement that any manufacturer would have welcomed. The Montclair was positioned in a higher price territory than the Monterey, however, and the junior model continued to be emphasized.

In 1957, everyone's eyes were on the Turnpike Cruiser—a new and radical Mercury. Mercury's "dramatic expression of dream car design" entered as the top-of-the-line series with two- and four-door hardtops and a convertible. It had, Mercury

1955 Monterey sedan, $2400.

1956 Mercury Monterey Colony Park wagon, $2977.

1957 Mercury four-door Turnpike Cruiser, $3849.

thought, just about everything. There was the "skylight dual curve windshield"—the retractable, reverse-slanted rear window. There were dual air intakes over the windshield corners that housed little radio antennae. There was even a creatively named "Seat-O-Matic" device, which automatically adjusted the driver's seat to any one of 49 pre-set positions at the flick of a button. The Cruiser used push buttons to link up with the Merc-O-Matic transmission, as did Chrysler. The convertible was a replica of the 1957 Indy pace car, and so on. However, the Cruiser sold only 16,861 copies (only 1265 convertibles) and failed miserably. It was too highly priced, for one thing. While it could be said that kitsch was not kitsch but high style in the '50s, the Turnpike Cruiser was really too far out even then. Besides, it earned a reputation for flunking the test on half of those fancy electronic maneuvers after a few thousand had hit the streets.

For the rest of the line, 1957 brought a major redesign on a new 122-inch wheelbase. A full range

Mercury

1958 Mercury Park Lane two-door hardtop, $3867.

1959 Mercury Monterey two-door sedan, $2768.

of Montereys and Montclairs were offered. Station wagons were placed in their own separate series, offering no fewer than six models. There was a Colony Park four-door nine-seater; a Voyager, of the same configuration plus a two-door; and three Commuters with the various seat and door combinations. It was a complicated group indeed, but was fairly successful. Mercury sold over 36,000 station wagons in 1957.

The Big M had grown a bit heavy-looking by '57, with big, oblong bumpers up front. The Turnpike Cruiser, with quad headlights, looked even heavier. The 312 V8 had grown commensurately, and now offered up to 290 hp. Similar styling, though slightly quieter, was offered for 1958. That year was a disaster. From 275,000 sales in 1957, Mercury fell to 128,000. The only consolation for Mercury was that Edsel was doing even worse.

Mercury made the Turnpike Cruiser an upperclass model of the Montclair in 1958. The Medalist was back for a short encore, with two- and four-door sedans again attempting to extend the price field downward to as low as $2547. Again, the Medalist was a disappointment: only 18,732 sold. Up in the higher brackets over the Montclair came the new Park Lane hardtops and convertibles, ostensibly to replace the Turnpike Cruiser with styling that was less outlandish. Park Lanes used the 430 cubic-inch Lincoln V8. The same brace of station wagons were offered, and a new automatic called Multi-Drive was available.

What had happened was that the bottom was gone from the middle-priced basket. A thinning-out was in progress. This is evident from the fact that Mercury didn't lose its position in 1958, but retained eighth place with only 40 percent of its 1957 volume. But significantly, an independent from Kenosha had passed Mercury in sales and was gaining fast on Pontiac, Olds and Buick. The Rambler revolution was underway. In its wake, Mercury would never be the same.

A little more of the same old stuff had to be cleared out before Mercury joined the rush to compacts and intermediates. Accordingly, the 1959s were given a severe face lift that resulted in a more conventional full-width grille and an extension of the odd concave rear fender styling of 1957-58. The Medalist and the Turnpike Cruiser were blessedly forgotten as the line thinned to four: Monterey, Montclair, Park Lane and Station Wagon. Even these survivors were severely cropped. The Montclair was down from six models in 1958 to just four, and there were only four varieties of wagons for 1959. Retrenching, Mercury built 157,000 cars, which was an improvement. But this production rate was only good for a ninth-place finish in '59.

A new Mercury engine for 1959 was the 383 cubic-inch V8—same displacement as Chrysler's, but more oversquare with a bore and stroke of 4.30x3.30 inches. The engine, standard equipment in the Montclair and station wagons, produced up to 322 hp. Montereys continued to rely on the 312 V8, which offered up to 280 hp.

History has dealt harshly with the Mercury (and Lincoln) of the late 1950s. Hindsight is a great advantage: the problems of the car were not as evident during its design evolution.

MERCURY AT A GLANCE 1950-1959

Model Year	1950	1951	1952	1953	1954	1955	1956	1957	1958	1959
Price Range, $	1875-2560	2189-2759	2191-2834	2194-2826	2194-2776	2218-2844	2254-2977	2576-4103	2547-4118	2768-4206
Weight Range, Lbs.	3321-3626	3485-3800	3335-3795	3335-3795	3435-3735	3450-3780	3430-3885	3870-4240	3790-4605	3914-4535
Wheelbases, Ins.	118	118	118	118	118	119	119	122	122, 125	126, 128
8 Cyl Engines, BHP	110	112	125	125	161	188, 198	210-235	255-290	235-360	210-345

Nash

**Nash Motors Division of Nash-Kelvinator, Inc.,
Kenosha, Wisconsin
American Motors Corp., Kenosha, Wisconsin**

It looks positively awful now, but the Nash Airflyte of 1949-51 was one of the most advanced cars of its day. It bristled with unusual features, and in shape it was as purely aerodynamic as a postwar car ever became. Though all manufacturers had toyed with similar shapes, only Nash actually put one into production.

The Airflyte began during World War II. Nils Erik Wahlberg had been a Nash engineer ever since the founding of the company in 1916. Ted Ulrich, who'd been a unit-body exponent since the 1930s, had helped create the 1941 Nash while he was at Budd Inc., the body builders. The '41 was the first successful mass-produced unit-body car. The success of that automobile led to Ulrich's hiring by Wahlberg.

Actual styling of the Nash Airflyte is claimed with some authority by Holden Koto, who, with partner Ted Pietsch, showed a small scale model very much like the eventual Airflyte to Wahlberg in 1943. Wahlberg must have been interested because he had been experimenting with wind tunnel tests on streamlined bodies. The ultimate Airflyte drag characteristics were superior: only 113 pounds of drag at 60 miles per hour, compared to as much as 171 pounds for the similar-looking 1949 Packard.

At the height of the seller's market, these Nashes sold very well; better, in fact, than any big cars in Nash history. For 1950, the sales figure was 191,865—an all-time Nash record. For 1951, with demand satiated, Nash built a total of 161,140 cars of which 57,555 were Ramblers. Two distinct Nash series were the Statesman, on a 112-inch wheelbase; and the Ambassador, on a 121-inch wheelbase. They were identical on the inside, but different outside from the cowl forward. The Ambassador used a longer, overhead-valve 234.8 cubic-inch Six; the Statesman used an L-head Six of 184 cubic inches. The latter engine, destroked to 172.6 cubic inches, also powered the Nash Rambler. Respected since its debut as an L-head in 1928, Ambassador's seven-main-bearing Six had one of the longest runs in history. It was not dropped until 1956. The Ambassador Six developed 115 horsepower; the Statesman, 85; the Rambler, 82. Each of the larger lines came in Super and Custom trim versions, in two- and four-door sedans and a club coupe. Statesman DeLuxe business coupes were sold at $1633 in 1950 and $1841 in 1951, making them the lowest-priced "bathtub" Nashes.

The little Rambler, riding on a 100-inch wheelbase, was the very antithesis of the huge Airflyte. Though there had been compact cars long before World War II and there were many unsuccessful

1950 Ambassador Super four-door sedan, $2064.

1950 Nash Rambler Custom Landau convertible, $1808.

attempts at them afterward, the Nash Rambler was the first postwar compact car to sell at really high volume. It was the progenitor of an entirely new breed of American automobile. Ford and Chevrolet had experimented with and discarded compacts right after the war, but the position of their small cars was fundamentally different from Nash's. George Romney, former AMC president, said, "It's one thing for a small company—a marginal firm—to pioneer a new concept like that and really push it. But it's another thing for people who already have a big slice to begin pushing something that undercuts their basic market.

Small cars fascinated Nash-Kelvinator's president George Mason. Mason was one of the most foresighted automotive executives of the postwar era. He knew that to ultimately survive after the seller's market ended, independents needed cars that the Big Three didn't offer. Together with Meade Moore, Nash's chief engineer, Mason kept hammering away at it until the Rambler was a reality. It arrived just as the sell-anything era was coming to a close, and held Nash's head above water until the company became American Motors

Nash

and began concentrating strictly on Ramblers after 1957.

The first-generation Rambler spanned model years 1950-52. In its first year, it was sold as a two-door station wagon and an interesting landau convertible. On the convertible, the window frames were permanently fixed; and only the top collapsed. A Country Club hardtop was added in 1951, but most of the sales came from the practical, attractive wagons. In those early days of the all-steel station wagon, Ramblers accounted for 22 percent of American sales for that body type.

Road tester Tom McCahill admired Mason and Nash tremendously. They were, he said, "busier than a mouse in a barrel of hungry cats" with their many projects. Yet another project was the Nash-Healey sports car—product of Nash cooperation with Donald Healey of Warwick, England. Mason and Healey met on the Queen Elizabeth in the mid-Atlantic, had a few drinks and concocted the Nash-Healey formula: a British-bodied sports car bearing some Nash identification on a 102-inch wheelbase, using a tuned Ambassador six-cylinder engine.

A look at Nash-Healey's prices from 1951 through 1955 show that the cars were not cheap, but they certainly were worth the money. A sports car in the true sense of the word, the N-H was competent on the track as well as on the highway. Production was miniscule: 104 units for 1951; 150 for 1952; 162 for 1953; and 90 for 1954, after which some Nash-Healeys were given 1955 serial numbers. A coupe joined the convertible for 1953. In 1954-55, that coupe was the only model available, restyled with a wraparound rear window.

Back where production really counted, sales of the bathtub had slowed. Last of that type was the '51, easily recognizable by its prominent rear fenders (1949-50 cars had rounded, bustle backs). For his 1952 redesign, Mason went to Pininfarina, and the result was a much nicer-looking if less aerodynamic Nash. The new, squared-off '52 line included the 114.5-inch-wheelbase Statesman and the 121.5-inch-wheelbase Ambassador. Both models retained the unit body. The Statesman engine was raised to 195.6 cubic inches and 88 horsepower.

The story was much the same in 1953. Identification of the new cars as 1953 models was provided by the small chrome spacers on the cowl airscoop. Once again the Statesman engine received a boost, this time to 100 bhp. Ambassadors offered a "Le Mans" option based on the latest Nash-Healey engine: the power plant produced 140 hp at 4000 rpm, through dual carburetors and a high-compression aluminum head.

An attractive new "floating" grille was adopted for the 1954 models. The lineup, however, was

1951 Nash-Healey, which sold for $4063.

1952 Statesman Custom sedan, $2332.

1953 Ambassador Custom Country Club hardtop, $2433.

1954 Rambler Custom convertible, $1980.

much the same as it had been in 1952-53. One difference was the deletion of two-door sedans from the two Custom series. Dual carbs and high compression had been successful on the Ambassador, so the same route was followed with respect to the Statesman in '54. The L-head was raised to 110 hp, and the setup was known (with a furtive look to Chrysler) as "Dual Powerflyte." Nash probably got away with using the Chrysler name only because Nash sales were so dismal. From the heady years of 1950-51, they'd dropped steadily: 152,000 in 1952; 135,000 in 1953; 63,000 in 1954. And a growing portion was accounted for by Rambler.

For 1955, the big Nash appeared with inboard headlights, which were an easy way to make the car look different, and added a V8 engine. Cooperation between the newly formed American Motors Corporation and Studebaker-Packard Corporation resulted in AMC's use of the Packard-built, 320 cubic-inch V8. The Ambassador Eight was much quicker than the Six, and cost $300 more. The Ambassador Six continued to use the ohv engine and offered the Le Mans power pack. The Statesman continued with its own L-head Six. Each series came in two models only—a four-door sedan and a Country Club hardtop.

After Hudson joined Nash in AMC, 1955 Ramblers were distributed to Hudson and Nash dealers alike with the appropriate grille badge. The model line-up grew to include the DeLuxe, Super and Custom sedans, hardtops, and Cross Country or Suburban wagons. A longer Rambler with a wheelbase of 108 inches was also added. This was not a model of Nash or Hudson, so it is covered in the Rambler section of this book.

The big Nash continued to be deemphasized. The last Statesman, a four-door sedan, appeared in 1956. Ambassadors all used the Packard V8 early that year, and switched to a 190-hp engine of 327 cubic inches in April. Cars with the larger power plant were called Ambassador Special.

For 1957, Nash mounted the headlights back on the fenders and fielded only two models, the Ambassador Super and the Custom. The latter was

1955 Statesman Custom Country Club, $2495.

1956 four-door Ambassador Custom, $2950.

1957 Ambassador Custom Country Club, $3100.

heroically overdecorated. A faster 327 V8 was used. The engine developed 255 hp with the help of four-barrel carburetor, dual exhausts and 9:1 compression. The styling was pretty good by contemporary standards, and the cars were among the first to offer four headlights as standard, but the big Nash was running out its last year. AMC was only slowly recovering from the debts forced on it through the merger and subsequent reorganization. Romney, who succeeded Mason as of Mason's death in 1954, pinned his hopes on the Rambler.

NASH AT A GLANCE 1950-1959

Model Year	1950	1951	1952	1953	1954	1955	1956	1957	1958	1959
Price Range, $	1633-2223	1841-4063	2003-5868	2003-5899	1550-4721	1457-5128	2146-3072	2820-3100		
Weight Range, Lbs.	2430-3390	2420-3445	2420-3550	2550-3550	1803-3575	1803-3839	3199-3854	3639-3722		
Wheelbases, Ins.	100-121	100-121	100-121.25	100-121.25	100-121.25	100-121.25	114, 121.25	121.25		
6 Cyl Engines, BHP	82-115	82-125	82-125	85-140	85-140	90-140	130, 135			
8 Cyl Engines, BHP						208	190, 220	255		

Nash Metropolitan

Nash/American Motors
Via Austin Motor Co.,
Longbridge, England

Big George Mason loved small cars. The Rambler was his first; the Nash Metropolitan followed. Before the Metropolitan ended its production run in 1962, nearly 95,000 of the little wonders had been sold. But Mason died in 1954, before the Metropolitan reached the height of its success.

The Metropolitan's origins go back to just after World War II, when Mason and engineer Meade F. Moore accepted a design by independent stylist Bill Flajole. Over a Fiat 500 chassis and drive train, a prototype was built and labeled NXI (Nash Experimental International). Mason had George Romney display the NXI at a variety of private showings in 1950, carefully sizing up public reaction before moving ahead with production. Reaction was favorable, but Mason still moved slowly: it wasn't until the end of 1953 that arrangements for volume production were complete. Metropolitan bodies were built in England by the well-known Birmingham manufacturers Fisher & Ludlow, Ltd. Bodies were then shipped to Austin at Longbridge, where the 42-horsepower engines were installed. The A-40 power plant was a Four with a displacement of 73 cubic inches. Met 1200s were introduced in early 1954 with a hardtop priced at $1445 and convertible at $1469. All were two-toned in happy colors resembling, as one writer put it, Neapolitan ice cream. Sales took off and Austin shipped 13,905 cars during late 1953 and 1954. Mid-year 1956 saw a more powerful Metropolitan 1500 with an engine of 90 cubic inches and 52 horsepower. Met 1500s used different paint combinations, a larger clutch and a new oval grille bearing Nash or Hudson emblems. The fake hood scoop that had adorned 1200s was dropped. Compared to about 70 mph for the earlier model, the 1500 would do close to 80, though not with sports-car efficiency. It was also higher priced, at $1527 for the hardtop and $1551 for the convertible.

Mid-year 1959 brought more refinements, though the 1500 designation remained. Mets received real

1954 hardtop which sold for $1445.

1957 1500 convertible, priced at $1591.

trunk lids for the first time. Prior to this, cargo was stored behind the seats. Comfortable seats, wing vents and tubeless tires were other improvements. Prices had risen to over $1600, but the Metropolitan was nevertheless enjoying its best year ever. With 20,435 built for calendar 1959, Metropolitan ranked second to Volkswagen among the imports. On its 85-inch wheelbase it was the smallest car sold by a domestic franchise, bar none.

Metropolitan production stopped in mid-1960, though leftovers accounted for 853 models in 1961 and 412 in 1962. Like many imported cars, it fell victim to the compact onslaught from the Big Three in 1960.

NASH METROPOLITAN AT A GLANCE 1950-1959

Model Year	1950	1951	1952	1953	1954	1955	1956	1957	1958	1959
Price Range, $					1445-1469	1445-1469	1445-1551	1567-1591	1626-1650	1626-1650
Weight Range, Lbs.					1803, 1843	1803, 1843	1803, 1843	1803, 1843	1835, 1875	1835, 1875
Wheelbases, Ins.					85	85	85	85	85	85
4 Cyl Engines, BHP					42	42	42, 52	52	52	52

Oldsmobile
Oldsmobile Division of General Motors Corp., Lansing, Michigan

Of all American automobile manufacturers remaining in operation today, Oldsmobile is the oldest. The story began when Ransom Eli Olds resolved to build "One carriage in as nearly perfect a manner as possible." That was back in 1897. In September 1908, William Crapo Durant formed General Motors, and a month later he absorbed Oldsmobile. But it wasn't until 1942 that the name of Olds Motor Works was changed to Oldsmobile Division of GM.

From the late 1930s on, Oldsmobile earned a reputation as the technological leader at GM. Olds introduced Hydra-matic on its 1940 models, built GM's first all-postwar automobiles in 1948, and offered the modern overhead-valve Rocket V8 engine in 1949. Olds was among the first GM divisions to offer wraparound windshields, four-door hardtops and four-door hardtop-wagons in the 1950s. And the '50s was a very good decade. The division built as many as 643,000 cars a year. In 1954 and 1958, Olds ranked fourth in production, behind Chevrolet, Ford and Plymouth.

The Futuramic styling of the 1950-51 Oldsmobiles could be traced back to prewar renderings and clay models, which emerged (with Cadillac) on the 1948 Olds 98. Smooth, low and streamlined compared to the upright GM styles of the past, it was extremely well received and soon influenced the entire GM line. On other makes it was not known as Futuramic, of course, but the Olds designation adequately described it. Olds restyled in 1952 and again in 1954, but the basic design concept—pronounced fenders and prominent grilles—remained a feature of the cars through 1956.

The last year for the L-head Oldsmobile Six (76) was 1950. After that year, all '50s models were powered by V8s. The Rocket 88 engine introduced in 1949 was another industry landmark. Designed by Gilbert Burell, it (and Cadillac's design) was a pioneer V8. Today, most large American cars are powered by engines like it. The Rocket had a displacement of 303.7 cubic inches from 1949 through 1953, though by '53 horsepower had risen to as high as 170. The power plant's compression ratio varied between 7.5:1 and 8:1, but the engine was capable of much more—up to 12:1 if the octane was available. A tremendously strong engine, the Rocket boasted a five-main-bearing crankshaft, oversquare bore and stroke of 3.75x3.44 inches, and great torque of 240 foot-pounds initially. Originally, Olds planned to use the Rocket only in the 98. But Sherrod Skinner, division general manager, had the brilliant idea of putting it in the lighter 88 too. The results were amazing. Olds 88s became NASCAR racing champs from 1949 through 1951.

1950 Series 76 club sedan, $1745.

1950 Series 88 Holiday hardtop, $2162.

1951 Super 88 convertible, $2673.

Weighing 300 to 500 pounds less than the 98, the Rocket 88 was an obvious NASCAR competitor. It scored early. Of nine NASCAR grand nationals held in 1949, 88s won six, with "Red" Byron the national champion. In 1950, an 88 broke its class speed record at Daytona with a two-way average of 100.28 mph. The same year, it was the winner of the first Mexican Road Race, besting such formidable competitors as Alfa Romeo, Cadillac and Lincoln. On the ovals, Oldsmobiles won 10 out of 19 races in 1950; the following year, they won 20 out of 41. Though displaced by the Hudson Hornet in 1952-54 stock car racing, 88s continued to show their ability

Oldsmobile

in other competitions. Paul Frére, for example, won the 1952 Francorchamps stock car race in Belgium with one—and a 1950 model 88 nicknamed "Roarin' Relic" was still winning the occasional modified race as late as 1959.

Such goings-on naturally helped keep Olds sales high after the seller's market began to shrink around 1950. Olds sold about 397,000 cars that year; during 1951-53 it did less well, but never fell below seventh place in production. By 1954 it was running fourth and had even passed Plymouth. Interestingly, Olds managed such sales triumphs with only three basic series, and didn't even have a station wagon between 1951 and 1956.

For 1950, with the 76 still in the lineup, there was only one 88 range. Standard and DeLuxe trim versions were offered at prices between $1878 and $2662. They included sedans; the club coupe; Holiday hardtop; wagon; convertible; and the last of Olds' special "club sedan," a four-door fastback. The 98 also came as a standard or DeLuxe in notchback and fastback sedans, Holidays and convertibles. All three '50 convertibles—the 76, 88 and 98—curiously were placed in the "standard" category: there were no DeLuxe versions. Their sales rate was not high: 973 of the 76s were sold; 9127 of the 88s; 3925 of the 98s.

For 1951, the Super 88 arrived on a new 120-inch wheelbase and with revised styling. The 88 line shrank to sedans only; the 76 vanished; and the 98 was offered as four-door sedan, Holiday hardtop and convertible. The all-steel wagons which Olds had featured during 1949-50 were dropped. They'd never sold well. Styling for '51 was only a bit gaudier than before. The grille was formed by simple bars, side decoration was minimal, and taillights were built into little upright fins on the rear fenders. The same basic styling continued on the nearly unchanged '52s, though the 88 moved up to the 120-inch wheelbase.

Along with Cadillac's Eldorado and Buick's Skylark in 1953, Oldsmobile offered a limited-production convertible. It was called Fiesta. Selling for $5715, Fiesta featured a custom leather interior, panoramic windshield and special 170-hp version of the Rocket V8. Standard power features included Hydra-matic, power brakes and steering, and hydraulic servos for windows and seat position. Fiesta's spinner wheel covers were soon copied by every accessory house in the business, and appeared on hot rods and custom cars from coast to coast. But only 458 Fiestas were produced, and the car was discontinued for 1954. Yet it had predicted a host of styling features to come, and 170 horsepower was merely the lowest output of an Olds engine in '54.

1953 Fiesta 98, which sold for $5715.

1954 Series 88 sedan, priced at $2334.

1955 Series 98 Holiday four-door hardtop, $3140.

The 1954-56 period marks another styling generation and some of the most attractive Oldsmobiles of the 1950s. Each series offered the same body styles in all three years, with the addition of four-door hardtops for 1955-56. A popular feature that had been introduced in '54 was "Autronic Eye," Oldsmobile's novel self-dimming headlight system.

The wheelbase for 1954-56 was 122 inches for the 88s and 126 for the 98s. All cars of the period used a bored-out engine of 324 cubic-inch displacement and 3.9x3.4-inch bore and stroke. Tuning the engine for various models gave it 170 hp in the basic 88, and 185 hp in the Super 88 and 98 during 1954. By 1956, as the horsepower race continued, the Olds figures were 230 and 240.

Oldsmobile built a record number of cars in 1955,

nearly 50 percent more than it had in 1954, but finished fifth because Plymouth had recovered. The 1954 line was retained, although it was drastically face-lifted with a new grille and two-tone color combinations. Together with Buick, Olds introduced the four-door hardtop, a design that was destined to be one of the most popular body styles of the late 1950s. By 1956, all of GM was offering this body, having planned for it well in advance. The rest of the industry hurried to put hastily contrived copies into production. Four-door hardtops generally were given to admitting rain and dust into the interior as the rubber window seals began to wear, but the idea of a four-door sedan with the airiness of a hardtop attracted buyers anyway.

The same approach was used in 1956. Most of the restyling occurred up front, where the cars had a large gaping grille derived from the Starfire show car. The division did exceptionally well in '56, producing 433,000 vehicles and maintaining fifth place.

Then came the '57s—all new designs and expanded series including the reborn station wagon. Once again Oldsmobile was innovative: some of those wagons were also four-door hardtops. The 88s of 1957 were labeled Golden Rockets, after another show car; the 98s were called Starfires. Station wagons, called Fiestas, came with and without door pillars in the 88 line; pillarless only in the Super 88 line. Standard horsepower was 277, but a popular option was the famous J-2 Rocket engine with three two-barrel carburetors and 300 horsepower. The J-2 was sufficient to propel an 88 from 0 to 60 mph in less than eight seconds. For a 1957 GM car, the Oldsmobile was rather cleanly styled—indeed, a bit stodgy. The gaping oval grille continued, only mildly reshaped. A broad, stainless steel spear dropped down from the middle of the beltline and shot straight back to the fenders to delineate the two-toning area. GM cars, in the face of Virgil Exner's Chrysler designs, were acquiring a reputation for old-fashioned styling, and the age of Harley Earl was quickly coming to an end. Nevertheless, Oldsmobile built 390,000 cars and held onto fifth place again.

In recession year 1958, while most of the industry faltered, Olds ran fourth and held production to over the 300,000 mark. Body offerings for 1958 were identical to those of 1957, except that two-door sedans were limited to the standard 88 series only. The styling, most observers concluded, was atrocious. Ford's Alex Tremulis satirized the '58 Olds rear fender and its four chrome strips by drawing in a clef and a few notes of music. Indeed, Fords were styled better than the GM cars; and the Chrysler Forward Look was in another league entirely. But Oldsmobiles still managed to sell well, aided, no doubt, by their potent engines. A 371 cubic-inch V8 had been introduced in '57, and by 1958 the hottest version was producing 312 hp.

Behind the scenes in Detroit and Lansing, big

1956 Series 88 Holiday hardtop, $2671.

1957 Starfire 98 Holiday four-door hardtop, $4013.

1957 Super 88 Fiesta, priced at $3541.

1958 Dynamic 88 Holiday four-door hardtop, $2971.

changes were being contemplated to keep Oldsmobile in the black. For the first time, cross-pollination was about to occur: the divisions were to share basic body shells. A new greenhouse design, using wide wraparound windows front and rear plus narrow pillars, was devised for all makes.

Oldsmobile

1959 Dynamic 88 Holiday Scenic hardtop, $2958.

1954 Starfire show car with namesake.

1956 Olds Golden Rocket.

Inner panels were shared between Chevrolet and Pontiac, and between Oldsmobile and Buick. Chevys rode the shortest wheelbase, while Olds and Buick shared two chassis with wheelbases of 123 and 126 inches. Pontiac was slightly shorter. Only Cadillac retained its own individual panels. Exterior styling for each division was developed enough to make the cars look different from each other, though there was more resemblance between the Olds and the cheaper Pontiac than Oldsmobile management would have liked. Pontiac surged past Oldsmobile in production for 1959, something it hadn't done since 1953.

Body sharing had other repercussions. Chevrolet, for example, had to drop its 1958 tooling, which was only a year old. Oldsmobile's former body had only two years behind it. Still, it was an effective move by GM's management, because the body sharing held big-car production costs down, and the company was able to put that much more time and money into its compacts. Oldsmobile would follow its peers into small-car territory with the F-85 in 1961.

The '59s, however, were big, roomy cars that offered high performance but low economy. Engines ranged from the 88's 371 cubic-inch unit with 270 or 300 horsepower to the new 394 V8 for the Super 88 and 98 that provided 315 hp with 9.75:1 compression and four-barrel carburetor. Performance, of course, was an Olds tradition.

Compared to Buick, '59 Oldsmobile styling was sedate. The grille was a rather plain oval with four widely set headlights; the tail angled upward to modest fins. The usual vast array of colorful interiors in vinyl and jacquard was offered.

As the innovator among GM divisions, Oldsmobile led in introduction of dream cars during the 1950s. After the semiproduction Fiesta came a series of two-seaters. The '53 Starfire was Corvette-like, incorporating a grille design taken from the Air Force's Starfire fighter. The grille eventually made its way onto the 1956 production cars.

Perhaps the most exotic Olds show car, though, was the 1956 Golden Rocket, a wild-looking aerodynamic coupe made of fiberglass and equipped with a 324-horsepower Rocket engine. Its features included roof panels that rose when the door was opened, swivel seats, running lights in plastic fins behind the doors, and a tilting steering wheel. Many Olds dream features ended up on competitive cars from Ford and Chrysler. That's not surprising because there were so many of them.

OLDSMOBILE AT A GLANCE 1950-1959

Model Year	1950	1951	1952	1953	1954	1955	1956	1957	1958	1959
Price Range, $	1719-2772	2049-3025	2262-3229	2262-5715	2272-3249	2297-3276	2422-3740	2733-4217	2772-4300	2837-4366
Weight Range, Lbs.	3260-4150	3507-4107	3565-4111	3603-4453	3699-4193	3688-4159	3691-4325	3963-4572	3972-4391	4040-4485
Wheelbases, Ins.	119.5, 122	119.5-122	120, 124	120, 124	122, 126	122, 126	122, 126	122, 126	122.5, 126.5	123, 126
6 Cyl Engines, BHP	105									
8 Cyl Engines, BHP	135	135	145, 160	150-170	170, 185	185, 202	230, 240	277-300	265-312	270-315

Packard

Packard Motor Car Co., Detroit, Michigan
Packard Division of Studebaker-Packard Corp., South Bend, Indiana

The Packard epic ended sadly in 1958, when the marque expired as a gussied-up Studebaker. The cars started out as heavy vehicles of no redeeming stylistic value in 1950, were transformed into crisp new modern shapes in 1951, and soared to the heights of luxury by 1956. The glorified "Packardbakers" of 1957-58 weren't much by comparison, but as Studebakers they set a fairly high standard.

The styling generation of 1948-50, known as the "pregnant elephant" by comics and Packard executives alike, was almost forced on the company by a chain of unavoidable events. Just before World War II, Packard introduced the very advanced and good-looking Clipper line of envelope-bodied sedans and coupes. The war stopped production almost as soon as it had started. When car production resumed in 1945. Packard followed the rest of the prewar companies in offering the same basic styles again. But most of the others had a good deal more production behind their prewar designs, and were able to retool for brand-new postwar cars for 1948-49. Most were ahead of the Clipper in appearance. Though Packard came out of the war in good

financial condition, the company was too small to simply throw the Clipper dies away. They had not been amortized by sufficient production.

The design that emerged in 1948 was therefore a face lift, not a restyling. Attempting to follow the apparent trend, Packard stylists loaded extra sheet metal onto the Clipper, eliminating the separate fenders and narrow, tapered hood/grille. The results were the ungainly 120-inch and 127-inch-wheelbase 1948-50 Eights, Super Eights and Custom Eights. As automotive writer Tom McCahill put it, they looked like they were meant to be driven "by a dowager in a Queen Mary hat."

Packard made another mistake just after the war: it continued to sell a line of medium-priced cars at $500 or so under the cheapest Cadillacs and Lincolns. This course reflected prewar decisions to build the volume One Twenty and One Ten, cars that saved Packard's life in the depression. After the war, though, the company could sell anything it cared to put on wheels. Yet Packard's reputation had been built on high-priced cars, and most historians agree that the company's decision to keep offering cheap models ultimately proved fatal.

Custom sedan and convertible, top-line 1950 models.   Prices: $3975 and $4520.

1951 Patrician/300/200 Deluxe sedans.   Prices: $3662, $3034 and $2616.

Packard

Cadillac and Lincoln began to sell volumes more high-priced cars than Packard, and by 1952 the company was holding only 3 percent of the luxury market.

None of this suggests that the elephants weren't good automobiles. Packard engineering has always been rated highly, and these cars were beautifully engineered, with big, smooth, low-revving straight Eights and roadable suspensions. Ultramatic, Packard's automatic transmission introduced in mid-1949, was the only automatic developed by an independent without outside help. While the seller's market lasted, it didn't make any difference whether a Packard sold for $2500 or $4500, and the firm could sell every one it could build. Production rose to nearly 105,000 in 1949 —the second-best year in company history.

Packard finally managed a total restyling for 1951, utilizing Packard designer John Reinhart's praiseworthy designs on 122- and 127-inch wheelbases. But Packard still persisted in building inexpensive cars. Its 200 series even included a business coupe at $2302 (the cheapest 1951 Cadillac was $2831), plus two- and four-door sedans in "basic" and deluxe trim. These 200s really weren't Packards in the traditional sense of the word, and when the seller's market subsided they weren't able to compete with established middle-priced rivals. Packard production dropped to 76,000 cars in 1951 and to less than 63,000 in 1952. Then the old management stepped down to let James J. Nance try to rescue the company.

The "real" Packards in 1951-52 were the 250s, 300s and 400s—all well-built, comfortable, high-speed road cars. The 250s used the shorter 122-inch wheelbase to mount the Mayfair hardtop and 250 convertible. These were luxuriously trimmed, colorful, sporty cars that sold fairly well. The 300 and 400 series were 127-inch wheelbase sedans. Packard's Patrician 400 was its highest-priced car in these years.

The expensive Custom Eight of 1950 had used a mammoth 356 cubic-inch straight Eight that weighed 1000 pounds. The smooth, nine-main-bearing engine developed 160 horsepower. It was considered too expensive to build in the light of potential sales, however. The top engine for 1951 was a 327 cubic-inch Eight—also with nine bearings and almost the same horsepower.

The Packard line for '52 was basically unchanged, though the 200 business coupe was dropped, fortunately. Styling changes were minor: the most obvious was a switch in the wing position of the pelican hood ornament. The colorful interiors of high quality fabric and leather were done up by fashion designer Dorothy Draper. Power brakes were offered for the first time.

1952 Patrician 400, $3797.

1953 Caribbean. Price: $5210.

1954 Convertible, $3935.

In May 1952, Hugh Ferry, Packard's aging president, announced the arrival of his successor, James J. Nance, and it was hoped that this market-wise promoter could invigorate Packard. By the time Nance arrived, the Packard plant was working at only 50 percent of capacity.

Incredibly, several long-time executives felt this was good enough, but Nance could see then what we all can see in retrospect: at that pace, Packard was doomed. He aggressively sought U.S. military business and laid out a vigorous new auto policy. Nance said the cheap 200s would be called Clippers and eventually would become a separate make. That they did, by 1956. Nance also said Packard would go back to building nothing but luxury cars, returning to the long-wheelbase formal sedans and limousines that it had neglected. This also happened.

There was no time for a complete line-wide change in the '53s, but Nance did see to the inclusion of eight-passenger sedans and limousines.

He even contracted with the Derham Body Company to build a few formal Patricians with leather-covered tops and tiny rear windows. The Patricians were priced at $6531 a piece. The glamorous Caribbean convertible was introduced with handsome styling and a 180-hp engine. Limited to 750 copies, it was well received and outsold Cadillac's comparable Eldorado. A colorful Clipper Sportser coupe was added to the bottom line.

Nance had hoped for an all-new 1954 line, but time didn't permit this. A look-alike series was offered, one that was outwardly distinguishable by horn-rimmed headlamps, and back-up lights built into the taillight assembly. The straight-eight Patrician engine was enlarged to 359 cubic inches to provide 212 horsepower; the 327s produced 165 to 188 hp. Even the lowest-priced Clipper's 288 cubic-inch engine developed 150 hp. Packard had been among the first to introduce air conditioning in 1940, and it was back in '54 for the first time since the war.

Packard had a terrible year in 1954, producing only 27,593 cars. Nance had wanted to introduce the revolutionary new model his firm was developing, but it was delayed. One reason for the delay was the hubbub caused by the so-called Packard-Studebaker merger. Actually, Packard bought Studebaker. What Nance didn't know when he signed the papers was that Studebaker had huge productivity problems in its high-overhead South Bend plant. The plants' break-even point was somewhere over 250,000 cars. Contrary to many accounts, Packard was still healthy at this time; Studebaker was sinking and would drag Packard down with it.

As the '55s neared production, another smouldering problem burst into flame. Packard had given away its body business to Briggs in 1940; in 1954, Briggs sold out to Chrysler. Chrysler told Nance it could no longer build his bodies, and Packard had to settle for a cramped plant on Conner Avenue in Detroit. Never big enough, the plant caused big production line tie-ups and quality control problems. Though Packard built nearly 70,000 cars in prosperous 1955, the company would have done better to consign body production back to its old but adequate main plant on Detroit's East Grand Boulevard.

Despite all these woes, the 1955 Packard was a technological wonder. Leading the list of features was Torsion-Level suspension, an interlinked torsion-bar system operating on all four wheels. A complicated electrical system allowed the suspension to correct for any load, and the interlinking of all four wheels provided truly extraordinary ride and handling.

There was more to the '55 picture, however. The old-fashioned straight Eights were superceded by powerful new V8s. These oversquare, very powerful units displaced 320 cubic inches on Clipper DeLuxe and Super, and 352 cubic inches on Clipper Customs and Packards. Ultramatic was also improved, to better deal with the higher torque. Combined with the V8 and Torsion-Level suspension, it was a fine drive train. Caribbeans, with four-barrel 352s belting out 275 horsepower, were impressively fast and roadable cars—Packards in every sense of the word. Styling also was excellent in '55. A clever face lift of the old 1951 body, the 1955 Packard sported "cathedral" taillights, peaked front fenders and an ornate grille. The Clipper was given its own special grille and 1954-style taillights, and therefore looked different from other Packards.

Some problems of the Conner plant were finally licked, but not in time to save the 1956 Packards. Studebaker's desperate struggle was scaring customers away. Also, many people refused to buy '56 Packards because of the notorious quality and service problems of the '55s. That was a shame, because the '56 models were better. Ultramatic was given new electronic push-button controls, and engines were increased in horsepower. The Clipper, as a separate make, was given the 352 cubic-inch engine; the Packard engine was bored out to 374 cubic inches, producing 290 hp in Patrician sedans and the 400 series hardtops, 310 hp in Caribbeans. There was a hardtop as well as a convertible Caribbean. Both had unique reversible seat

1955 Clipper Custom Constellation hardtop, $3076.

1956 Four Hundred hardtop.   Price: $4190.

Packard

1957 Clipper town sedan, $3212.

cushions—fabric on one side, leather on the other. In mid-year, a Packard Executive appeared in sedan and hardtop form, bridging the gap between Packard and Clipper on the 122-inch wheelbase. Executives wore Clipper's pointed taillights and Packard grilles. But none of this product shuffling helped. Only 10,317 Packards were built for model year 1956.

No financial backer was found for an all-new 1957 line, and Nance finally resigned. Studebaker-Packard was picked up by Curtiss-Wright Corporation as a tax write-off, and C-W's Roy Hurley began directing the firm's fortunes. Late in 1955, the firm decided to leave Detroit and to build Studebaker-based Packard cars in South Bend.

The 1957 "Packardbaker" was, despite it all, a very good Studebaker too, though hardly in the image of the Packards that had gone before. A sedan (120.5-inch wheelbase) and a station wagon (116.5-inch) were offered. A supercharged Studebaker 289 V8 provided 275 horsepower, the same as some previous Packard V8s. Styling evoked Packard themes, and the cars were priced much higher than comparable Studebakers. It was a charade, of course, and the public recognized it: only 3940 Packard Clipper town sedans were built, along with 869 country sedans (wagons).

1958 Hawk hardtop, $3995.

A big-Packard revival was still possible as the '58s were planned, so Studebaker-Packard tried the same holding action again. This time, four Studebaker-based cars were marketed at prices between $3212 and $3995. On the shorter wheelbase came a two-door hardtop and wagon; a sedan and the Packard Hawk used the longer wheelbase. The latter, most famous of this generation, was a more luxurious version of the Studebaker Golden Hawk. It had an all-leather interior and bizarre styling. In defense of Duncan McRae, its stylist, the Packard Hawk was really built only because of Roy Hurley. It was Hurley who demanded the long, bolt-on fiberglass nose and gaudy gold mylar tailfins. McRae, however, takes credit for the car's strange outside armrests. McRae was also forced

1958 Hardtop, priced at $3262.

to create the other three 1958 Packards—garish, finned affairs with hastily contrived four-headlight systems designed to keep up with the competition. Production figures were: 159 wagons, 588 Hawks, 675 hardtops, 1200 sedans. Only the Hawk retained the supercharged engine.

After the '58s were gone, the Packard name ceased to appear on automobiles, although the corporation continued to use the name until 1962. Then the company became simply Studebaker.

PACKARD AT A GLANCE 1950-1959

Model Year	1950	1951	1952	1953	1954	1955	1956	1957	1958	1959
Price Range, $	2224-4100	2302-3662	2494-3797	2544-6531	2544-6100	2586-5932	3465-5995	3212,3384	3212-3995	
Weight Range, Lbs.	3815-4620	3550-4115	3640-4100	3700-4720	3585-4720	3670-4755	4045-4590	3570,3650	3470-3555	
Wheelbases, Ins.	120-141	122,127	122,127	122-149	122-149	122,127	122,127	116.5,120.5	116.5,120.5	
8 Cyl Engines, BHP	135-160	135-155	135-155	150-180	150-212	225-275	275-310	275	225,275	

Plymouth

**Plymouth Division of Chrysler Corp.,
Detroit, Michigan**

Plymouth's evolution in the 1950s closely followed that of its rival, Chevrolet. Plymouth started into the decade as a producer of economical, no-nonsense transportation in 1950, but fielded one of the "hot" cars of 1955. By the '60s, the company had an expanding line of increasingly luxurious and expensive automobiles. The division's cars had no real style at all in 1950, but developed into some of the most stylish cars in America after 1956.

These design and engineering revolutions were prompted by Plymouth's declining fortunes between 1950 and 1954. From 1931 up to that time, the division had never been challenged as the number-three producer behind Chevrolet and Ford. But in the early '50s, Plymouth built fewer and fewer cars; it dropped to fifth place in sales for 1954.

The Plymouths of 1950-54 were well engineered, solid and reliable—but not fast or stylish. All of them were powered by the same engine. Chrysler Corporation's smallest L-head Six, displacing 217.8 cubic inches and with a bore and stroke of 3.25x 4.38 inches, produced 97 horsepower at 3800 rpm through 1952. Output was raised to 100 hp in 1953 (probably by the stroke of an ad writer's pen), and to 110 hp in 1954. The engine was capable of 20 to 23 miles per gallon, and perhaps 80 mph if pressed hard enough. (Interestingly, this long-lived L-head lasted through 1959, after which it was replaced by the modern overhead-valve slant-six. But Plymouth did get the L-head up to 132 hp by the end of the decade.)

In 1950, there were two lines—the DeLuxe and Special DeLuxe. The Special outsold its stablemate by about seven to five. DeLuxes offered basic four- and two-door sedans, club and business coupes, and a pair of steel-bodied station wagons. The Special DeLuxes came as sedans, club coupes, convertibles and wood-bodied station wagons that were the last of Plymouth's woodies. The cars incorporated two important innovations in the low-priced field: the automatic electric choke and the combination ignition/starter switch.

Plymouth had built about 575,000 cars in 1949 and in 1950. For 1951, it built 621,013 cars using a new design. The '51s were a little less blunt at the front end. New model names also helped to make the line appear fresh. There were Concord two-door sedans, coupes and wagons; Cambridge four-door sedans and coupes; and Cranbrook sedans, coupes, hardtops and convertibles. The Cranbrook hardtop, christened Belvedere, was Plymouth's first hardtop, and arrived a year behind Chevrolet's. The Belvedere was distinguished from

1950 DeLuxe business coupe, $1386.

1951 Concord fastback sedan, $1688.

1951 Cranbrook sedan, $1841.

1952 Cranbrook Belvedere hardtop, $2231.

Plymouth

other Plymouth models by a two-tone paint scheme. It attracted many buyers in 1951 and 1952.

Plymouths, like other Chrysler Corporation cars, remained essentially unchanged for 1952. The easiest way to tell the '52s from the '51s is by looking at the rear. The '52s have the Plymouth name integrated with the trunk handle assembly; the '51s spell it out in a separate piece of script. One important improvement on 1951-52 models was the Oriflow shock absorber—a Chrysler hydraulic type that was designed to improve ride and handling. Plymouth made about 175,000 fewer cars in 1952 than it did the year before; but the rest of the industry also cut back production that year because of the Korean War, and Plymouth remained the number three producer.

Plymouth adopted flow-through fenderlines and the one-piece windshield for its redesigned 1953 models.

Previous Plymouths had used two wheelbases—111 and 118.5 inches—but all the '53s rode a 114-inch wheelbase. The Concord was dropped, so the Cambridge series expanded to include business coupes and wagons. Late in the year, only a handful were built: 2240 four-door sedans, 760 club coupes. Another midyear introduction was Hy-Drive, a combination manual transmission and

torque converter. It made second-to-third shifts unnecessary, but the driver still had to declutch to get off the line in first gear. Hy-Drive was a follow-up to overdrive, which Plymouth had introduced on the 1952 models. The '54s would also utilize two-speed PowerFlite automatic, which was very popular.

Plymouth, and Chrysler cars in general, suffered in 1954 as a result of their uninspired styling. Fewer than 400,000 Plymouths were built. Plymouth rearranged its model lineup in 1954. Plaza, Savoy and Belvedere spanned the price gap between $1618 and $2288.

These models would be offered again in 1955, but with a dramatic difference: in '55, Virgil Exner's all-new styling made Plymouths exciting cars to look at, and a brand-new polyspherical-head V8 made them good performers as well.

The 260 cubic-inch "Hy-Fire" V8 was an excellent engine in the small-displacement generation that began with Studebaker's 232 V8 in 1951. With a bore and stroke of 3.56x4.63 inches, it produced 157 horsepower in "economy" guise; 167 hp as "standard"; and 177 hp with four-barrel carb and dual exhausts. The engine's outstanding features included lightweight aluminum pistons, an aluminum carburetor, and chrome-plated top piston rings for longer life and better oil control.

Other new mechanical features for 1955 were dashboard-controlled PowerFlite, suspended foot pedals, tubeless tires and front shocks enclosed

1953 Cambridge club sedan, $1727.

1955 Belvedere sedan V8, $2082.

1954 Belvedere Sport Coupe.   Price: $2145.

1956 Belvedere V8 Sport four-door hardtop, $2385.

74

within the coil springs. For the first time, Plymouths could be had with air conditioning, power windows and power front seats. Brisk new pointed-end styling and neat two-toning characterized the three-model lineup. The Belvedere group offered a sporty hardtop and convertible. The convertible was available only with a V8 engine in '55 and throughout the rest of the 1950s. "A great new car for the young in heart," it was called — a total departure from the past. Plymouth built 742,991 cars in '55, a 12-month record that would still stand in the 1970s. Even so, Plymouth ranked only fourth — behind Chevy, Ford and Buick.

In 1956, Virgil Exner formally announced The Forward Look, which meant tailfins. Plymouth Engineering simultaneously brought forth push-button PowerFlite, 12-volt electrics, and an optional Highway Hi-Fi record player that used special records designed to keep the needle in the groove. A new Suburban line covered four different wagons: two- and four-door models in standard and special trim. A four-door hardtop was added to the Belvedere series; a two-door hardtop was added to the Savoy.

The hottest performance news was the limited-production Fury — an attractive hardtop painted white, with gold anodized body stripe. The Fury featured a 303 cubic-inch version of the V8, giving 240 hp at 4800 rpm. The Fury engine used 9.25:1 compression cylinder heads, solid lifter cam, stronger valve springs, dual exhausts and Carter four-barrel carburetor. It approached 145 mph on test at Daytona Beach, and would do 0 to 60 in 10 seconds. Its top speed in standard form was 111 mph. The Fury contributed greatly to the growing Plymouth performance image, and the company sold 4485 of them — not bad for a car priced $500 higher than a Belvedere hardtop.

If 1955 had seen a numerical victory with record production, 1957 saw a moral triumph. Plymouth returned to third place. Over 655,000 cars were built that year. The fresh new designs by Virgil Exner prompted Plymouth's ad men to exclaim, "Suddenly it's 1960." Compared to their rivals, the Plymouths probably were three full years ahead. They had the lowest beltlines, the most glass, the cleanest looks and the highest tailfins in their field. They rode on a 118-inch wheelbase (wagons were 122 inches), and were more powerful than before. The old L-head Six now ground out 132 hp, the Hy-Fire V8 delivered up to 235 hp, and the Fury's new 318 engine delivered 290 hp. Like other Chrysler cars they featured torsion-bar front suspension, with revised suspension geometry to make them the best-handling, best-riding Plymouths ever.

Now 20 years later, it's hard to remember how truly revolutionary the '57 Plymouths were at the time. The roofline, for example, was so clean and delicate-looking that it did not appear to serve any structural purpose. The grille, usually a large ornate object in those days, was slim and graceful on

1956 Fury Sport hardtop, priced at $2866.

1957 Fury Sport hardtop, $2925.

1957 Belvedere V8 sedan, $2410.

1958 Sport Suburban Six, six-passenger. Price: $2760.

the Plymouths. Its height was reduced by a raised bumper that rode over a separate stone shield. At a time when rival cars were often garishly two-toned, Plymouth settled for a slim sweep of contrasting color along the sides to match a duo-tone roof. Solid colors were offered, or sometimes only the roof was two-toned. Traditional pillar sedans offered huge glass areas; the V8 Belvedere convert-

Plymouth

1959 Sport Fury hardtop. Price: $2927.

1958 Cabana show car with sliding sunroof.

ible's windshield curved around the top, as well as the sides. By midyear, there was a four-door hardtop in the Savoy line as well as the Belvedere. All hardtops had beautiful interiors of jacquard and vinyl. Dashboards grouped all instruments in a bolt-upright pod directly in front of the driver, and knobs and other controls were located safely out of the way. Suburbans saved space by placing the spare tire in a rear fender—a design first seen on the Plainsman show car of 1956. The '57s were memorable cars. They are rare today because of a proclivity to rust.

Plymouth's 1958 line closely followed the successful '57s, except that four headlamps were used and a new front stone shield did away with 1957's vertical slots. Engine horsepower of the V8 was up to at least 225, and as much as 315 in the high-performance Fury. Instant recognition at the rear was provided by round taillights. The space above them was filled by a piece of bright metal. During the recession, Plymouth built only 367,000 cars, but everyone else was affected too. The division remained third overall in production.

Plymouth's tailfins grew in '58 as big as they'd ever get, and they were not very pretty. Front ends received a more garish, egg-crate grille and a flatter hood; and the sides of the cars were decorated with anodized silver panels. The low-priced Plaza line vanished. The remaining model names were Savoy, Belvedere and Fury. The Fury became a volume range, offering a four-door sedan and hardtop as well as a two-door hardtop. To retain the individual features and high performance of former Fury cars, Plymouth introduced the custom Sport Fury. Priced at $2927 to $3125, these two-door hardtops and convertibles were the top of the '59 line. They were equipped as standard with a 260-hp version of the 318 V8; for $87 extra, buyers could get a new 361 Golden Commando V8 that produced 305 hp at 4600 rpm.

Plymouth built 413,204 cars in 1959 and held third place, but a new rival was coming on strong.

Rambler rose to number three in sales for 1960-61; after that, Plymouth was held back by Pontiac. Not until 1970 did Plymouth rank third again.

Plymouth show cars of the 1950s were unique and interesting. The XX-500 of 1951 was a Ghia exercise—a very pretty sedan that won Ghia the patronage of Exner for show cars and limousines to follow. Ghia also built the Plymouth Explorer of 1955, a fast, smoothly styled grand tourer. A Briggs project was the Belmont sports car of 1954, which suggested there might be a Plymouth two-seater (built by Briggs) to compete with Corvette and Thunderbird. Limited 1955 sales of the latter two models caused the company to drop this idea, however. Dream cars lending new ideas to production were the wagons: Plainsman in 1956, Cabana in 1958. The Plainsman was marked by lots of glass like that of Chevrolet's Nomad, and the aforementioned spare-time compartment. The Cabana sported even more glass and four-door hardtop treatment. Neither configuration saw production, mainly because of cost.

PLYMOUTH AT A GLANCE 1950-1959

Model Year	1950	1951	1952	1953	1954	1955	1956	1957	1958	1959
Price Range, $	1386-2387	1552-2237	1625-2344	1618-2220	1618-2288	1639-2425	1784-2866	1899-2925	2028-3067	2143-3131
Weight Range, Lbs.	2872-3353	2919-3294	2893-3256	2888-3193	2889-3186	3025-3475	3030-3650	3155-3840	3170-3840	3130-3805
Wheelbase, Ins.	111, 118.5	111, 118.5	111, 118.5	114	114	115	115	118, 122	118, 122	118, 122
6 Cyl Engines, BHP	97	97	97	100	110	117	125	132	132	132
8 Cyl Engines, BHP						157-177	180-240	197-290	225-315	230-305

Pontiac

Pontiac Division of General Motors Corp., Pontiac, Michigan.

Of the four new makes introduced by General Motors prior to the Great Depression, only Pontiac survived. Buick Division's Marquette line, Cadillac Division's LaSalle, Oldsmobile Division's Viking and Oakland Division's Pontiac were the new entries. The first three were short-lived, but the Pontiac line soon began to outsell all other Oakland cars and Pontiac itself became a GM division. Following World War II, Pontiac set many new records. It reached third place behind Chevrolet and Ford by 1962. The division faltered in the late 1950s, but its setbacks were temporary.

Usually, Pontiac built the right cars at the right time. When buyers began passing up six-cylinder medium-priced cars, Pontiac wisely forgot them. At the height of the horsepower race, Pontiac produced the Bonneville. For most of the '50s, the division maintained competitive prices. This helped Pontiac win sales, especially from Plymouth and Dodge.

Pontiacs of the early 1950s offered six- or eight-cylinder engines in a wide variety of body styles. In 1950 there were two- and four-door sedans, business and club coupes, all-steel wagons, hardtops, convertibles, and two- and four-door fastbacks called Streamliner sedans.

The engines were robust L-heads. The Six originally displaced 239.2 cubic inches and delivered 90 horsepower. Its output was gradually increased to 118 hp by its last year, 1954. The Eight displaced 268.2 cubic inches and yielded 108 hp in 1950, but by 1954 was putting out up to 127 horsepower. Both engines disappeared when the V8s arrived.

The '50 styling was a face lift of 1949 designs created by Harley Earl's Art and Colour Studio. All Pontiacs used the famous Silver Streak hood applique that dated back to before the war, and the illuminated countenance of Chief Pontiac as a hood mascot. Virgil Exner had created the Silver Streak. It remained a Pontiac styling feature through 1956—a run of 22 years. All 1950 models offered optional Hydra-matic drive at a price of $158. This was also the first year for a Pontiac hardtop, the Catalina. Four varieties of Catalina were offered, and by the end of the year they were accounting for 9 percent of production.

Although 1951 proved less successful in terms of volume, it was by no means disappointing to Pontiac. Car output that year was the second-best in the division's history. (On August 11, the four-millionth Pontiac was built.) The Streamliner fastback four-door sedan, which had been the sole holdover of that style from 1950, was dropped in the spring of '51. The cars for '51 were altered little from those of the year before, but did get a new

grille with a "V" motif. The trend toward Eights continued.

Pontiac dropped its coupe bodies in 1952, reducing both Six and Eight series to sedans, four-door wagons, Catalinas and convertibles. Within each range there were still three separate trim series, however: the Chieftain, DeLuxe and Super DeLuxe. This year was the last for the 1949 Earl styles. They were replaced for 1953 by a new Chieftain Six and Eight on a 122-inch wheelbase. Korean War restrictions and a nationwide steel strike slowed 1952 production to 277,000 cars, but Pontiac remained in fifth place.

Trends were discernible as the 1953 models made their debut. Catalina hardtops, for example,

1950 Eight Deluxe sedan. Price: $1908.

1951 Eight Catalina hardtop, $2257.

1952 Chieftain Deluxe sedan. Price: $2015-$2090.

Pontiac

were accounting for over 20 percent of volume, and Hydra-matic installations had climbed to 84 percent. The 1953 models bore a distinct resemblance to earlier body styles, though they were larger in almost every dimension. New features were the kicked-up rear fender line (Pontiac fenders had tapered downward in the past), lower and more streamlined grille, upright-winged "Chief" hood ornament, and one-piece windshield. Mechanical improvements included optional power steering. Pontiacs equipped with Hydra-matic had an especially low rear axle ratio of 3.03:1. This gave them smooth top-range performance and increased the appeal of Pontiac's shiftless transmission. A fire in the Hydra-matic plant in mid-1953 shortened the supply of this unit, however, so about 18,500 Pontiacs were fitted with Chevrolet Powerglide in '53 and '54. Pontiac did extremely well for calendar year 1953, producing 414,000 cars.

The 1954 models were face-lifted '53s, with revised side molding and a narrow scoop built into the central grille bar. They included the new luxury Star Chief, in sedans, hardtops and convertibles that were priced between $2301 and $2630. Production reached 371,000 units for the year.

A big change was hinted at in early 1954. It was Pontiac's first V8. The new engine was known as Strato Streak. It produced 180 horsepower, or 200 hp with the optional four-barrel carburetor. Initially, it displaced 287.2 cubic inches; but it was capable of enlargement, and it soon grew to over 300 cubic inches. A lively, strong, conventional design with five main bearings, it was up to date, over-square—3.75x3.25-inch bore and stroke—and ran on regular gas with an 8:1 compression ratio.

There was more to 1955 than the new engine. Pontiac claimed 109 new features altogether, including extensively revised styling and an improved chassis as well as the V8. Pontiacs came in Chieftain and Star Chief series; they featured wrap-around windshields, a cowl ventilation system, new colors and two-toning, tubeless tires, and 12-volt electrical systems. The 122-inch-wheelbase Chieftain range comprised an 860 series of sedans and wagons, and an 870 line of sedans, wagons, and the Catalina hardtop. The 124-inch wheelbase Star Chief offered four-door sedans and convertibles as standard plus another sedan and Catalina as Custom.

Included in the Chieftain 870 range was the exotic new hardtop-styled Safari two-door wagon, based on the Chevrolet Nomad. Carl Renner, Chevrolet stylist, said: "When Pontiac saw [the Nomad] they felt they could do something with it . . . Management wanted it for the Pontiac line—so it worked out." Safaris were built with Nomad-hardtop styling through 1957. They were priced

1953 Chieftain 8 Custom Catalina hardtop, $2446.

1954 Star Chief Custom Catalina hardtop, $2557.

1955 Star Chief convertible, $2691.

1955 Safari, priced at $2962.

higher than Nomads, of course, and sold in fewer numbers: 3760 in 1955, 4042 in 1956, and 1292 in 1957.

On balance, 1955 must be rated a vintage year for Pontiac. The division built a record 581,860 cars in the 12 months. Though Pontiac had been passed by Oldsmobile in 1954 and ranked sixth in '55, the

1956 Chieftain Custom Safari, $3129.

1957 Pontiac Bonneville, $5782.

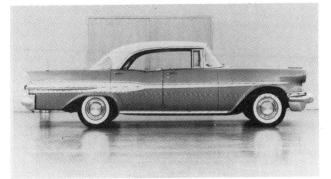

1957 Star Chief Catalina sedan, $2975.

1958 Bonneville Custom Sport coupe, $3481.

Pontiac lineup was a solid hit with the public and the dealers. But Pontiac had some rough times in the later 1950s. The division didn't hit its 1955 volume again until 1962, after which it began setting records again. Pontiac didn't continue at its previous half-million-unit level because of changes in the automotive market. Buick's Special and

Oldsmobile's standard 88 were more competitively priced than they'd been before. Moreover, the market for cars in the lower-medium price range was shrinking as the imports steadily increased their share of American sales. Pontiac did not seem to capture the enthusiasm of buyers in the 1956-58 period, even though its cars were radically altered through most of these years, and were faster than ever.

A mild face lift and the addition of four-door hardtops marked 1956, but only 332,000 cars were built. Styling was less distinctive than it had been in 1955. (Tom McCahill said the '56 looked like "it had been born on its nose.") Though the V8 was displacing 316.6 cubic inches it didn't pack an extraordinary amount of power—only 227 hp maximum in the Star Chief. Also, the cars had picked up a reputation for a hard ride.

GM appointed Semon E. "Bunky" Knudsen general manager of Pontiac, told him to do what he could with the old bodies, and hoped for the best in 1957. Knudsen hustled. Though given the same wheelbase of the year before, 1957 Pontiacs had very long rear springs mounted in rubber shackles. Ball-joint front suspension, adopted by other GM Divisions, was ignored, however. New 14-inch tires replaced the 15-inchers. A foot pedal parking brake and an automatic radio antenna that came up when the set was switched on were new features for '57. The massive buck-toothed grille was revised. Two-toning departed from its half-a-car 1956 pattern, and moved to a simpler sweep-spear motif.

All Pontiacs received a new 347 V8—and here Bunky had his day. He gave us the fast and flashy Bonneville.

Providing 310 horsepower by way of fuel injection, hydraulic lifters and racing cam, this $5782 convertible was the fastest Pontiac in history. It was even faster with the optional Tri-Power (three two-barrel carbs) instead of fuel injection. A fuel-injected Bonneville was tested at 18 seconds for the standing quarter mile; one with Tri-Power did the same leap in 16.8. Fuel injection never proved popular, and was soon dropped by GM. Bonnevilles weren't hot sellers at that price—only 630 were sold—but they did impart a whole new performance image to the division. Corporate racing was being played down, however. A few '57 Pontiacs raced with distinction in NASCAR, but they were strictly private entries.

Yet the lack of race results didn't affect Pontiac sales in 1957. Chevy, Olds and Buick all suffered downturns from 1956 (as Chrysler products filled the gap), but Pontiac built about 343,000 cars and moved to within 10,000 units of Olds.

The revised styling for 1958 should have brought Pontiac added success, but the recession set in and held the division's production to only 220,000 units. The cars really were well styled. A simpler, full-width grille was adopted, and the side spear was widened slightly. Bodies were lower, but not

Pontiac

much longer or wider; wheelbases were unchanged. No fewer than seven Catalina hardtops were offered with two or four doors. Bonneville became more of a volume car, selling 27,128 convertibles and hardtops.

For 1959—the division sharing inner body shells with Chevrolet, Buick and Olds—new styling made Pontiacs some of the best-looking cars around. The first of the famous split grilles was introduced, along with modest twin-fin rear fenders and minimal side trim. The V8 was pushed up to 389 cubic inches, and with Tri-Power it delivered 315 hp. Pontiac also made a new Tempest 420E unit for economy-minded buyers. It developed 215 hp and could deliver 20 miles per gallon if driven prudently. The old Chieftain and the Super Chief had been discontinued and replaced by the Catalina on the shorter wheelbase; the Star Chief and Bonneville shared the 124-inch wheelbase. Bonneville was a real hit, and 82,564 '59 models were sold. Pontiac built close to 390,000 units that year.

Pontiac produced a number of interesting one-offs. The smooth-looking four-door hardtop Strato Streak was introduced in 1954, on the 124-inch wheelbase. It was a harbinger of pillarless four-doors to come in the 1956 model year. Also shown was the first Bonneville, a fast Corvette-like two-seater with a canopy-type cockpit and a 100-inch wheelbase. Both of these cars were fitted with straight Eights. The Strato-Star of 1955 boasted a 250-hp V8. Strato-Star was a two-door, four-seat hardtop that provided a preview of 1956 styling. Metallic silver paint and a red leather and brushed aluminum interior were featured, as was flow-through ventilation.

The wildest show car was the 1956 Club de Mer. It incorporated "twin pod" seating and dual windshields. It stood only 38.4 inches high. Painted Cerulean blue (Harley Earl's favorite color), the sports-car body was made of anodized aluminum. Its engine was a 300-hp V8, specially tuned.

1959 Catalina Vista. Price: $2844.

Experimental Strato Streak, a four-seater.

Bonneville Special show car with canopy top.

1956 Club de Mer with anodized brushed-aluminum body.

PONTIAC AT A GLANCE 1950-1959

Model Year	1950	1951	1952	1953	1954	1955	1956	1957	1958	1959
Price Range, $	1571-2411	1713-2629	1956-2446	1956-2664	1968-2630	2105-2962	2370-2857	2463-5782	2573-3586	2633-3532
Weight Range, Lbs.	3209-3689	3193-3698	3253-3688	3391-3716	3331-3776	3476-3791	3452-3797	3515-5425	3640-4065	3870-4370
Wheelbases, Ins.	120	120	120	122	122	122, 124	122, 124	122, 124	122, 124	122, 124
6 Cyl Engines, BHP	90	96	100	115	115, 118					
8 Cyl Engines, BHP	108	116	118	118	122, 127	180, 200	205, 227	252-310	240-310	215-315

Rambler

**American Motors Corp.,
Kenosha, Wisconsin**

When George Romney succeeded George Mason as AMC president, Romney turned his full attention to the Rambler and soon forgot about proposed cooperation with Studebaker-Packard. The Rambler was AMC's most successful car, and was exploiting a whole new market.

AMC introduced a new, 108-inch wheelbase Rambler with Nash and Hudson badges in late 1955. A few months later, the 100-inch wheelbase Nash and Hudson Ramblers were phased out, and by 1957, the larger model carried only the Rambler name. The large car was a solidly built, reliable automobile, perfectly attuned to the new economy market. By 1961, its successor had brought Rambler to third place in the industry.

All but forgotten today is the fact that Rambler introduced the industry's first four-door hardtop-wagon: the 1956 Custom Cross Country. This neat, airy, roomy estate car was priced at $2494—about $170 above the standard Deluxe Cross Country. Like other Rambler wagons, it featured a 33 percent increase in cargo space over that of the '55s, and a roll-down tailgate window that eliminated the clumsy upper hatch. "We just rolled with those cars," said AMC Board Chairman Roy D. Chapin Jr. "We couldn't get enough." There was nothing like the luxurious little Cross Country, and the public responded accordingly. The 1956 line also included four-door sedans in DeLuxe, Super and Custom series, and a Custom four-door hardtop. They were all unit-body types. The DeLuxe sedan at $1829 was one of the lowest-priced cars in the country.

In 1957, with the big Hudson and Nash destined for oblivion, American Motors built 118,990 cars; 114,084 of them were Ramblers. Important changes occurred as the range expanded. The overhead-valve Six, which displaced 195.6 cubic inches, was raised to 125 and 135 horsepower from 120 in 1956. Also, a lively new V8 of 250 cubic inches was offered. The V8, a modern, oversquare engine (3.50x3.25-inch bore and stroke) produced 190 hp at 4900 rpm. It was available only on the upper-priced cars—Custom, and Super Sedan and wagon. An interesting new model in the Custom range was the specially trimmed Rebel. This four-door hardtop was announced mid-year with an even larger V8, the new AMC 327. The Rebel had Gabriel shocks, an anti-roll bar, heavy-duty springs, power steering and power brakes. All that and 255 horsepower from the 9.5:1 compression V8 transformed Rambler's image. During tests at Daytona Beach, a Rebel flew from 0 to 60 (and 50 to 80) in scarcely more than seven seconds. It also handled well. Unfortunately, it just didn't appeal to

the basic Rambler market, and only about 1500 were built. Priced at $2786, it was also the most expensive '57 Rambler, and that may have contributed to its low sales.

Economy cars continued to set sales records, so for 1958 AMC brought back the 100-inch models. Called Rambler Americans, and fitted with a new mesh-type grille, they sold for as little as $1775.

1956 Super sedan.   Price: $2123 to $2253.

1957 Rebel, priced at $2786.

1958 Rebel Custom, priced at $2457.

Rambler

Such prices couldn't help but sell cars, and 42,196 Rambler Americans were registered for the 12 months.

Larger Ramblers received more than 100 changes for 1958, and were outwardly quite different from their predecessors. The grille was made more massive and square; dual headlamps were used; fashionable little fins appeared at the rear; and pedal-type parking brakes were adopted. The archetypal Rambler, the six-cylinder Super Cross Country wagon, was the top seller in '58. The Rebel name was retained, incidentally, to designate cars powered by the 250 cubic-inch V8. But Rambler did not revive the fancy, limited-edition Rebel hardtop. Instead, it created a new 117-inch wheelbase for a line of cars powered by the 327 V8 and dubbed the line Rambler Ambassador.

Actually, Ambassador styling had been predicted in mid-1957, when it was thought that these cars would bear separate Nash and Hudson identification. In essence, they were enlarged versions of the accepted Rambler theme: roomy, squarish bodies available as four-door sedans and wagons, with or without roof pillars. The Ambassador hardtop wagon was the only one in the 1958 Rambler line. Only 294 were sold. In fact, Ambassador sales were quite disappointing—just 1340 for the model year. Ambassadors were entering a field of heavy competition and decreasing demand, and AMC did much better with its smaller Ramblers. Registrations of all Ramblers for 1958 climbed to 186,227—in a year that was generally a disaster for other manufacturers. After four years of losses, AMC turned the corner, making a profit of $26 million on sales of $470 million.

For 1959, it was the same formula again. This time the company netted $60 million in profits and built nearly 375,000 cars for an all-time record. The same models and power trains were offered, but horsepower wasn't raised. Unlike its competitors, AMC apparently decided enough was enough.

1959 Ambassador Custom four-door sedan, $2732.

1959 Rebel Custom, priced at $2588.

The Rambler American DeLuxe and Super lines acquired a new station wagon, helping rack up 90,000 sales for the junior series. The 108-inch-wheelbase cars were again mildly face-lifted with thin "color sweep" side molding and simplified grilles. As in 1958, Rambler V8s were called Rebels, and used the 250 cubic-inch engine. The Ambassador Super and Custom continued as before, with the longer wheelbase and a more ornate grille.

Limited success with the large Ambassador should have told AMC something. Big cars—even though their wheelbases were a few inches shorter than those of standard-size automobiles—were not profitable for the company. In the later 1960s, AMC reverted to its early policy of competing with the larger manufacturers on many price and size levels, with unpleasant results.

RAMBLER AT A GLANCE 1950-1959

Model Year	1950	1951	1952	1953	1954	1955	1956	1957	1958	1959
Price Range, $							1829-2494	1961-2786	1775-3116	1821-3116
Weight Range, Lbs.							2891-3110	2911-3409	2439-3586	2435-3591
Wheelbases, Ins.							108	108	100-117	100-117
6 Cyl Engines, BHP							120	125, 135	90-138	90-138
8 Cyl Engines, BHP								190, 255	215, 270	215, 270

Studebaker

Studebaker Corp., South Bend, Indiana
Studebaker Division of Studebaker-Packard,
South Bend, Indiana

In 1950, Studebaker was the oldest auto manufacturer, having been in continuous operation since the days of horse-drawn carriages. The company was enjoying its best year ever in 1950, and many grand predictions were made about Studebaker's upcoming "second century." But the company's United States operations came to an end just 12 years later, and its Canadian branch built the last Studebaker automobile two years after that.

The story of how this happened is complex, but it can be summarized as follows: (1) Studebaker's productivity was lower than that of the rest of the industry, even though the company's work force was highly paid; (2) the firm's old South Bend plant had a high overhead and was more isolated from component suppliers than were the factories in Detroit; and (3) the Big Three, competing among themselves, caused casualties among the independents—when Ford and Chevy started price wars, Studebaker dealers could not keep pace because of their lower volume.

The product itself probably had less to do with the firm's failures than most people think. Though Studebaker styling was controversial, it was usually predictive of similar ideas to come from other manufacturers. The bullet nosed 1950-51 models weren't really duplicated by anyone else, but they did suggest the strong central styling motif that was to appear later in different form on Edsels and Pontiacs.

The styling was the work of Raymond Loewy Associates, consultants to Studebaker since the late 1930s. The jet aircraft was Loewy's obvious inspiration. The frontal design of the 1950-51 Studebakers was radically different from that of the 1947-49 models, but from the cowl back they were all closely related. The '50 models also offered Studebaker's excellent automatic transmission, designed in cooperation with the Detroit Gear Division of Borg-Warner.

For 1950, Studebaker fielded a short-wheelbase Champion in three trim variations, powered by the 169.6 cubic-inch engine of 85 horsepower. Commanders rode a longer wheelbase and used a 245.6 Six of 102 hp. The long-wheelbase Land Cruiser was part of the Commander series, available as a four-door sedan only. The Champion engine continued for 1951, but the Commander received Studebaker's first V8.

Displacing 232.6 cubic inches, the new engine developed 120 hp at 4000 rpm. It was fairly conventional, though overhead cams and hemispherical combustion chambers had been considered. The 232 and its successors have been called heavy for their displacement. But such statements are unfair,

made on the basis of comparisons with designs that were developed much later, after significant improvements had been made in casting and foundry techniques. The Studebaker V8 was the first in a long line of robust, efficient power plants that displaced less than 300 cubic inches. Those that followed from Dodge, Ford, Chevrolet and Plymouth certainly benefited from the Studebaker's technology. Its greatest contribution, perhaps, was the elimination of the largest barrier between popular-priced cars and luxury machines. As a result, V8s would become the favored engines of Americans.

The '51 Studebakers were in essence the same line of cars that had been offered in 1950. As before, there was a six-cylinder Champion series in Custom, DeLuxe and Regal trim variations; and the larger, eight-cylinder Commander. The main difference in the lineup from '50 to '51 was that Studebaker had reduced the size of the larger body. Commanders for 1951 shared a 115-inch wheelbase with Champions, and the Land Cruiser's wheelbase

1950 Champion DeLuxe sedan, $1597.

1951 Commander State sedan, $2143.

Studebaker

dropped from 124 to just 119 inches. Prices went up slightly, but buyers seemed happy to pay the difference for the livelier V8, and this increased the Commander's sales considerably. The V8 was not a powerhouse, but it did give Commanders 90-mph performance. As time would tell, the engine was capable of considerable additional displacement and horsepower.

Styling changes for '51 were slight: the bullet nose was refined with a second chrome circle, and the prominent air vents above the grille were deleted. Model names were spelled out on the leading edge of the hood. Whatever can be said about its

1952 Commander State Starliner hardtop, $2488.

1953 Commander State Regal hardtop, $2374.

1954 Commander Regal sedan, $2287.

styling now, the bullet nose was apparently popular when new.

Selling 222,000 cars for calendar 1951, Studebaker fell far below its 1950 record; but this was more a result of Korean War restrictions than of decreased demand. Studebaker's share of the market actually increased in 1951, from 4.02 to 4.17 percent.

The company's centenary was marked in 1952. Though all-new styles weren't ready, the face lift was acceptably different. The bullet-nose was replaced by a low, toothy grille that some stylists called the "clam digger." The model lineup stayed the same, with the addition of the first Studebaker hardtop, the Starliner. But production was much lower throughout the industry and Studebaker built only about 162,000 cars. Optimistically, management looked upon the coming '53s with more enthusiasm.

The now-legendary "Loewy coupes"—Commander and Champion, Starliner hardtop and Starlight coupes—were actually designed by Robert E. Bourke, chief of the Loewy Studios at South Bend. Bourke had envisioned a special show model at first, but Loewy knew a good thing when he saw it, and sold the car to Studebaker's management. The sedans, which naturally had to adopt the same sort of styling, were somewhat less successful, but the coupes were truly magnificent. Mounted on the new 120.5-inch Land Cruiser wheelbase rather than the sedans' 116.5-inch wheelbase, the Starliner/Starlight was perfect from every angle. Not a line or a detail was out of place. It was hailed at the time as the "new European look." Today, it's considered by many the finest American automotive design of the entire decade.

Sadly, the changeover to these new cars delayed production, and Studebaker's output of 186,000 cars for 1953 was a disappointingly small improvement over 1952. Further errors surfaced when demand for Bob Bourke's coupe began running four times higher than that for the sedans. Management had planned just the reverse. More time was lost in switching over.

The same series of cars were offered for 1954 (an egg-crate grille is the most obvious addition), but production was worse, at only 85,000 units. By now the weaknesses of the company were becoming apparent, and the cost of building a car was frightening. As an experiment, Bourke "priced out" a Commander Starliner using the General Motors cost structure, and found that Chevrolet could have sold it for about $1900. Studebaker was selling it for $2502. The Ford Blitz was on, as Ford waged a price war with GM. Neither giant damaged the other, but both wreaked havoc on the independents. Just when things looked blackest, Packard bought Studebaker and announced a bold new effort to create "the industry's Big Four."

Unable to justify new 1955 styling so soon, Studebaker hung a lot of chrome on the old bodies and in mid-year adopted a wraparound windshield. The model line was shaken up, with Champions (including the hardtop) all based on the shorter wheelbase. The longer wheelbase now served two separate lines, the Commander and President. The Champion Six was raised to 101 horsepower. Curiously, the firm shrank the Commander V8 to 224.3 cubic inches, while getting 140 horsepower out of it. Presidents, in turn, used a larger V8: 259.2 cubic inches; 175 hp. The top of the line was the wildly two-toned President Speedster hardtop. It offered a special quilted-vinyl interior; tooled metal dash; and color combinations like pink and black, or "lemon and lime." At $3253, it was not a seller. Neither were its line mates. In a year when nearly every company was setting new sales records, Studebaker produced only about 112,000 cars. Soon it was determined that the company needed to sell about 250,000 cars just to break even.

While Studebaker-Packard President James Nance shopped for finances (eventually leading to the Curtiss-Wright takeover), Studebaker gamely restyled for 1956. Retaining the old wheelbases, bodies became more upright and squared off, with larger, mesh-type grilles. A cheap two-door called the sedanet was offered in Commander and Champion lines. What was left of the long-wheelbase chassis was applied to the top-line President Classic sedan, and the sporty new Hawks.

The Hawks were the last Studebakers of the 1950s that were designed by Loewy's team. The Hawks were good-looking cars. They were exciting to drive, competent on the curves and impressive on the straightaway. There were four altogether. Descendants of the pillar-type Starlight coupe were the Power (V8) and Flight (Six) Hawks. Based on the old Starliner hardtop were the Sky Hawk and Golden Hawk. The latter ran a big, 352 cubic-inch engine provided by Packard. Hawk styling was keyed to a square, classic-style grille; freestanding parking lights; and deluxe interiors with turned metal dashes like those of the '55 Speedster. A Flight Hawk sold for less than $2000, and the Golden Hawk listed at only $3060, so they were good buys. Unfortunately, they were peripheral models that appealed only to enthusiasts, and Studebaker's bread-and-butter cars continued to sell only a few crumbs at a time. Only 82,402 vehicles were turned out in South Bend in 1956, and things would get worse. In 1957 and 1958, Studebaker and Packard combined couldn't produce more than 73,000 cars a year.

These were dog days at South Bend—a time when none of the plant's employees knew from one day to the next whether they were working on their last model. Stuck with the 1956 restyling there wasn't anything to do but conduct a face lift. A full-width grille appeared for 1957. That grille grew more massive in 1958, when the cars also gained hastily developed quad headlight systems and ungainly tailfins to keep up with the times. The Scots-

1955 President Speedster.   Price: $3253.

1955 Commander Regal station wagon, $2445.

1956 Golden Hawk hardtop, $3061.

1956 President Classic sedan, $2489.

1957 Commander DeLuxe, $2171.

Studebaker

1958 President hardtop, $2695.

man—a naked, bargain-priced line of two- and four-door sedans and a station wagon—did not spark sales. Neither did the nice-looking Starlight hardtop, with its De Soto-like roof.

Mechanical changes were, however, beneficial. The '56 Golden Hawk's huge Packard engine made the car embarrassingly front-heavy. So for 1957-58 the pretty two-door hardtop used a Paxton Studebaker V8 of 289 cubic inches, with Paxton supercharger. This arrangement developed the same 275 horsepower that the old Packard engine did, but in a much more efficient way: the blower freewheeled economically until the accelerator was floored. The other 1956 Hawks were replaced by a single Silver Hawk coupe that used plainer trim and an unblown 289 developing 210 horsepower. The Golden Hawk and Silver Hawk were fine road machines, capable of carrying four people comfortably over long distances at high speed in the true *gran turismo* tradition. As "personal cars," their appeal was limited, especially in 1958 when Studebaker hit bottom. Fewer than 50,000 cars were built that year.

For Studebaker, the end might have come right there, but another chance appeared in the form of the compact Lark. Though it used several inner panels and mechanical components from leftover models, stylist Duncan McRae had done enough to the exterior to make it look different. The boxy, practical styling found a market among compact-conscious buyers in 1959, and people flocked to Studebaker dealerships in droves. The turnaround was astounding. In model year 1958, for example, 18,850 four-door sedans had been built. The 1959 figure came to 48,459 four-door Larks. The '59 Lark series was composed of two- and four-door sedans, and two-door wagons and hardtops on a 108.5-inch wheelbase. The six-cylinder models still used the old L-head of 169.2 cubic inches, detuned to 90 hp. The V8-powered models were fitted with the 259.2 V8—rated at 180 hp, or 195 with four-barrel carburetor. In V8 form, Larks were lively and surprisingly easy on gas. The Hawk

1959 Lark Regal hardtop, $2275-$2410.

1959 Silver Hawk, $2360 to $2495.

was also continued for 1959, but only the Silver Hawk model was issued.

Studebaker made its first profit in six years in 1959, and built over 150,000 cars. The Lark had temporarily saved the company. Four years later, after limited resources had caused that same Lark to be offered for too long, Studebaker was back in trouble. Once again, limited-production personal cars, the Hawk and the Avanti, failed to solve the real problem: insufficient production of family cars. Thus the final Studebakers were built in 1966.

STUDEBAKER AT A GLANCE 1950-1959

Model Year	1950	1951	1952	1953	1954	1955	1956	1957	1958	1959
Price Range, $	1419-2328	1561-2481	1735-2548	1735-2374	1758-2556	1741-3253	1844-3060	1776-3182	1795-3282	1925-2590
Weight Range, Lbs.	2620-3375	2585-3240	2655-3230	2690-3180	2705-3265	2740-3275	2780-3395	2725-3415	2695-3470	2577-3148
Wheelbases, Ins.	113-124	115, 119	115, 119	116.5, 120.5	116.5, 120.5	116.5, 120.5	116.5, 120.5	116.5, 120.5	116.5, 120.5	108.5-120.5
6 Cyl Engines, BHP	85, 102	85	85	85	85	101	101	101	101	90
8 Cyl Engines, BHP		120	120	120	120	140, 175	195-275	180-275	180-275	180, 195

Willys

Willys-Overland Motors, Toledo, Ohio
Kaiser-Willys Sales Corp., Toledo, Ohio

Though more closely related to the Jeep family than to passenger cars, the Jeepster should be mentioned in any discussion of Willys in the 1950s. Designed by Brooks Stevens (of Excalibur fame) and based on wartime Jeep styling, this sporty convertible was produced for four model years. In the last two years, 1950-51, an egg-crate grille replaced the upright grille of 1948-49. The later vehicles were less luxurious, though no Jeepster was really deluxe. Jeepsters were at first powered by Willys L-head Fours and Sixes, which displaced 134 and 148 cubic inches. In mid-1950, the Four was converted to an F-head; the Six was enlarged to 161 cubic inches. Sixes became F-heads too, but not until 1952. Over 10,000 Jeepsters were sold for 1948. In 1950, however, only 4066 Fours and 1779 Sixes were sold, and some of them were leftovers registered as 1951s.

The 1952 Aero-Willys was a unit-body car styled by Phil Wright and engineered by Clyde Paton. Returning Willys to the passenger-car field, it was a clean design providing good comfort and handling.

Four separate series were offered for 1952. The Aero-Lark used the older, 75-hp L-head Willys Six; the Wing, Ace and Eagle hardtop ran the overhead-valve 161 Six. The 161 was small, but was a good performer, providing economy on the order of 25 miles per gallon. The biggest problem the cars had was their list price. An Eagle hardtop, for example, sold for $2155; a Chevrolet Bel Air hardtop cost $150 less than that. Willys-Overland dealers were hard pressed—not only to explain how builders of Jeeps could produce a smooth, comfortable family car, but also why they had to charge so much for it. Production was good, but not great. For the '52 model year, 31,363 Aeros were built. About 33 percent of them were base-line Larks: about 16 percent were Eagle hardtops.

Willys expanded the line for 1953, making only minor appearance changes including red-painted wheel cover emblems, and a gold-plated "W" in the grille to symbolize the firm's 50th anniversary. About 500 Larks used an F-head four-cylinder engine this time. It displaced 134 cubic inches and developed 72 horsepower. The Aero-Wing was replaced by the Aero-Falcon. A new four-door sedan was developed for the Lark, Falcon and Ace. These models ranged from $1646 for the least expensive Lark to $2038 for the four-door Ace. Again, the Eagle was priced on the high side at $2157. Willys-Overland had another modestly good year, selling 41,735 of the 1953 Aeros.

In 1954, Willys-Overland was purchased by Henry Kaiser, whose ailing Kaiser-Frazer Corporation was melded in to form the Toledo-based Kaiser-Willys

1950 Jeepster model: $1494-$1690.

1952 Aero-Lark two-door sedan, $1731.

1953 Aero-Ace two-door sedan, $2038.

1954 Aero-Eagle hardtop, $2411.

Willys

Sales Corporation. The K-F plant at Willow Run was sold to General Motors, and production was concentrated at the old Willys plant.

At first, the new 1954 Aeros appeared to be the same line of cars that had sold in 1953 with larger taillights and revised interiors. But in March 1954, the company made the 226 cubic-inch L-head Six available as an option on the Ace and Eagle. (To further complicate matters, there were Ace and Eagle "Customs"—with the latter designation merely indicating the presence of a "continental" exterior spare tire.)

Aeros powered by the Kaiser 226 were really fast automobiles, at least for Sixes. Though their top speed of about 85 mph was little higher than the cars equipped with Willys engines, they were geared for acceleration. And accelerate they did. A typical 0-60 time was 14 seconds. As an experiment a few cars were even fitted with the 140-bhp supercharged Manhattan engine, which engineers say gave acceleration times comparable to those of contemporary V8s.

The 1954 Aeros also handled much better than before. A new front end was adopted, using threaded trunions that were adjustable for wear. The kingpins and coil springs were longer, shocks and A-arms were stronger, and the steering idler arm was lengthened. A cross member connected left and right front suspension assemblies to eliminate lateral torque and reduce tow-in variations. The 1954 Aero-Willys was thus one of the best combinations of ride and handling produced by a domestic manufacturer in the 1950s. The Eagle hardtop in particular was an attractive car, though price was still a problem: '54 Eagles sold for up to $2411, or close to $2600 with Hydra-matic. Sales of 1954 models dropped to 11,875 units.

By early 1955, the decision was made to abandon passenger cars at Kaiser-Willys. But in the meantime, 6564 of the '55 Willys cars were sold. No longer called Aeros, the line was divided into the Custom two- or four-door sedans and the Bermuda

1955 Custom sedan, priced at $1795.

1955 Bermuda hardtop, $1895.

hardtop (plus 663 Ace sedans for export). Engine options included 161 and 226 cubic-inch Sixes. Prices were cut drastically in an effort to move them out. The Bermuda was advertised as the nation's lowest-priced hardtop, but too few people cared: only 2215 of them were built, and most of them were powered by the 226 engine.

Styling of the '55 models was much busier than before, and no designer takes credit for their looks. A clumsy attempt at two-toning involved complicated side trim. The grille was no longer a simple bar, but a garish expanse of concave, vertical bars. In contrast to this glittery model, a neat hardtop-wagon had been planned for 1955. So had a very sleek face lift for 1956. Neither materialized.

The Aero did get a reprieve south of the border. Its dies were eventually shipped to the former Kaiser subsidiary, Willys do Brasil. There, a cleaned-up '55 model without the busy side molding was built with F-head Willys engines through 1962. So the Aero actually lasted over 10 years—a fair run that attests to its basic good design.

WILLYS AT A GLANCE 1950-1959

Model Year	1950	1951	1952	1953	1954	1955	1956	1957	1958	1959
Price Range, $	1494-1690	1597-1703	1731-2155	1646-2157	1737-2411	1725-1895				
Weight Range, Lbs.	2392-2485	2459-2485	2487-2584	2487-2575	2623-2904	2751-2847				
Wheelbases, Ins.	104	104	108	108	108	108				
4 Cyl Engines, BHP	63, 72	72		72	72					
6 Cyl Engines, BHP	70, 75	75	75, 90	75, 90	90-115	90-115				

Minor Makes

Many small companies or small offshoots of larger companies produced cars of the '50s that were not discussed in the previous section of this book. Information about some of these little-known, low-production or one-off automobiles is sketchy at best, but we present here the data that we have been able to accumulate so far.

The dates given after the name of the car are those of initial introduction. Locations, when known, are given along with the name of the company. If the name of the company is the same as the car, the company name is omitted.

Aerocar, 1948. Longview, Washington. Combination of car and plane. The company is still in existence.

Andree Special, 1955. Location unknown. Formula 1 and 2 racing car. The car used Crosley hydraulic disc brakes, Volkswagen front end, and a tubular frame.

Argonaut, 1959. Cleveland, Ohio. Seven fine models, ranging from two-passenger coupes to limousines, on wheelbases from 126.5 to 154 inches. Bodies were aluminum. A V12 overhead-cam air-cooled aluminum engine was planned. The Argonaut claimed over 1000 horsepower, 13 miles per gallon, and up to 240 mph. A handful were built through 1963.

Arnolt, 1953. Chicago, Illinois. Built by S. H. Arnolt in 1953-54, the car used an MG chassis with open or closed Bertone body of aluminum. The price was $3585. About 200 were built.

Arnolt-Bristol, 1954. Companion to the Arnolt MG, built from 1954 to about 1964. The Arnolt-Bristol

1959 Asardo with fiberglass body.

used the 120 cubic-inch overhead-cam Bristol Six, a 130-hp engine. The cars finished 1-3-6 in their class at Sebring in 1960. Prices ranged from $4000 to $5000, and 142 were built.

Asardo, 1959. American Special Automotive Research & Design Organization, North Bergen, New Jersey. This sport coupe used a 91 cubic-inch, 135-hp Alfa Romeo engine; tubular space frame; and light fiberglass body. Speed of 135 mph was claimed. The price was $5875.

Ascot, 1955. Glasspar Co., Santa Ana, California. This fiberglass roadster sported butterfly-type fenders, square grille, and outside space. The Ascot used various engines including a Studebaker Six, and weighed 1770 pounds.

Astra-Gnome, 1956. Richard Arbib Co., New York. Futuristic prototype with custom body by Andrew Mazzard. Featured were fluted aluminum side panels, bubble cockpit canopy and "walk-in" entry.

Aurora, 1956. Branford, Connecticut. An experimental safety car built by Father Alfred A. Juliano, using a 1954 Buick chassis; Cadillac, Lincoln or Chrysler engine; fiberglass body. The car was to be a nonprofit venture, with proceeds going to safety research, but no production occurred. The estimated price was $15,000.

Auto Cub, 1956. Randall Products, Hampton, New Hampshire. A 51-inch-long runabout powered by a Briggs & Stratton 1.6-hp engine, the Auto Cub sold for just $169.50 and claimed 75 miles per gallon. It was a running mate of the 1956 Daytona.

Banner Boy Buckboard, 1958. Banner Welder, Inc., Milwaukee, Wisconsin. Using a Briggs & Stratton 2.75-hp air-cooled engine, Banner's car was similar to the B&S Flyer that was built in Milwaukee 25 to 30 years earlier.

Basson's Star, 1956. Basson's Industries, Bronx,

Arnolt-Bristol, companion car to the Arnolt.

New York. The final attempt to get the Martion Stationette on the road. The Star was a three-wheeler, powered by a one-cylinder, two-cycle engine. The price was $999.

BMC Sports, 1952. San Francisco, California. No connection with British Motors Corporation in England. This was a fiberglass sports car using the Singer 1500 engine.

Bocar, 1958. Denver, Colorado. The name is an acronym for builder Bob Carnes. The car used a fiberglass body on a tubular frame, with Chevrolet or Pontiac supercharged or fuel-injected engines. The price was $4146, plus engine. Performance was in the 175-mph range. Production continued until about 1960.

Buckboard, 1956. Automotive Assoc. Co., White Plains, New York. A two-passenger car with oak chassis, mahogany body and 43-hp Ariel motorcycle engine. All-wheel independent suspension and Renault steering were featured on a 94-inch wheelbase.

Buckaroo, 1957. Cleveland, Ohio. A small car with air-cooled motor, priced at $400.

Charles Town-About, 1958. Stinson Aircraft, San Diego, California. Conceived by Stinson's president Charles Graves, this was a 48-volt electric car with twin electric motors. It was capable of a top speed of 58 mph and a range of 77 miles. The body was a modified Karmann Ghia. The Van-About was a panel truck variation. Production continued into 1959.

Checker, 1959. Kalamazoo, Michigan, Checker was founded in 1922, but only began selling cars to the general public in 1959. Like Checker cabs, the first models used Continental 226 cubic-inch Sixes in L-head or overhead-value configurations. For 1965, Checker switched to Chevrolet Sixes and V8s. Checkers are still sold to the public in small quantities, but most are purchased by taxi companies.

Cheetah, 1952. Doug Coruthers, California. Coruthers was connected with the Skorpion project.

1956 Daytona, companion to Auto Cub, but bigger.

Cheetah was a fiberglass sports car using a modified Ford Chassis.

Chicagoan, 1952. Triplex Industries, Blue Island, Illinois. Two-passenger fiberglass sports car using Willys six-cylinder engine. Up to 15 cars were built through 1954.

Colt, 1958. Boston, Massachusetts, and/or Milwaukee, Wisconsin. A small, 700-pound two-seater priced at $995, it was powered by a one-cylinder, 23 cubic-inch Wisconsin air-cooled engine and could do 50 mph.

Cornell Liberty, 1959. Experimental safety car built for Liberty Mutual Insurance by Cornell Aeronautical Laboratories. It incorporated 90 safety features. The driver sat ahead of the passengers, and had 180-degree vision. Cost was $100,000.

Crofton, 1959. San Diego, California. A small, Jeep-type car with a Crosley engine. The car weighed 1100 pounds and sold for $1350. The Crofton Bug was built through 1961. A Brawny Kit added six-speed transmission, power-lock differential and other deluxe features for $1800. About 200 vehicles were built.

Custer, 1953. Dayton, Ohio. Exact date of start-up not certain. The Custer was a buckboard-type runabout that used electric motors capable of 18 mph or gasoline engines capable of 40 mph. The electric version had two forward speeds. Custers were still being produced as late as 1959 or 1960.

Darrin, 1955. Kaiser-Darrins powered by Cadillac V8 engines were sold by Howard Darrin at $4350.

Daytona, 1956. Randall Products. Hampton, New Hampshire. Companion to Auto Cub but larger, the Daytona could hold two passengers. It used a 7-hp Briggs & Stratton engine and sold for $495.

Debonnaire, 1955. Replac Corp., Euclid. Ohio. This sports-car kit on a Ford chassis was related to the Venture that was also made by Replac.

Devin, 1958. El Monte, California. Fiberglass

1959 Cornell Liberty, experimental safety car.

sports-car bodies, also available complete in 1959 with Chevrolet 283 V8s and chassis made in Ireland. Devin SS cars sold for $5950; kits for as little as $295.

Dual-Ghia, 1955. Detroit, Michigan. Short-lived but popular luxury GTs built by Gene Casaroll, based originally on the 1953 Dodge Firearrow show cars. Cars were assembled using various Chrysler components; the Dodge D-500 V8 engine was standard. Body styles included four-passenger convertible or hardtop on 115-inch wheelbase, priced from $7500 up. Between 104 and 117 cars were built through 1958.

Duesenberg, 1959. Detroit, Michigan. Only one was built, using a Duesenberg eight-cylinder engine rebored to 435 cid, developing 400 hp; Packard chassis; and steel and aluminum roadster body.

Edwards, 1949. South San Francisco, California. Sterling Edwards' ultimate sports car, first constructed in Culver City, California. It used a 107-inch wheelbase tubular chassis, aluminum body and Ford V8 engine. Later, Edwards used fiberglass bodies and Lincoln engines. The price was about $5000. The cars were built through 1955.

El Morocco, 1956. Detroit, Michigan. These were 1956-57 Chevrolet convertibles, restyled to resemble concurrent Cadillac Eldorados. Perhaps 30 were made. Surprisingly, they were sold at the same price as production Chevrolets.

Electronic, 1955. Salt Lake City, Utah. A sophisticated 110-inch wheelbase electric car, sometimes called La Saetta. Priced at $2995, it used a gas or diesel engine to generate power for an 80-cell battery hookup. This powered an electric motor within the rear axle housing. Only one was built.

Electric Shopper, 1956. Long Beach, California. Production may not have begun quite as early as '56, but it continued at least until the 1960s. It was a three-wheeled electric with a 61-inch wheelbase. The price was $750 for the metal body, $945 for the fiberglass.

Eshelman, 1953. Baltimore, Maryland. A one-passenger runabout using a 3-hp Briggs & Stratton engine, the Eshelman could attain 70 mpg with a top speed of 25 miles an hour.

Excalibur, 1952. Beassie Engineering Co., Milwaukee, Wisconsin. This was Brooks Stevens' sports-car adaptation on the Henry J chassis, using an Alfa Romeo or Willys engine. The Willys-powered cars would do up to 120 mph and were quite successful in SCCA racing, but intended production did not materialize. The estimated list price was $2000-$2500.

Fina Sport, 1953. New York, New York. A dream notion by a New York car importer, the Fina used a 115-inch wheelbase Ford chassis and a 210-hp Cadillac V8. The price was $10,000. Convertibles and hardtops offered.

Fletcher-Flair, 1954. Fletcher Aviation, Rosemead, California. A Jeep-type four-wheel-drive vehicle with a 1500cc Porsche engine and a 78-inch wheelbase.

Flintridge, 1957. Los Angeles, California. German DKWs with modified fiberglass bodies by Howard Darrin, Flintridges were priced at $3195.

Forerunner, 1955. A fiberglass body on the Jaguar XK-120 chassis, designed by Bill Flajole of Detroit. This was a two-passenger fastback with electrically operated plastic roof. It was said to be capable of 140 mph.

Frick, 1955. Rockville Centre, New York. With Ferrari-like, Vignale-styled body on a 110-inch wheelbase, the Frick used a Cadillac V8. A supercharger was optional.

Gaylord, 1955. Chicago, Illinois. An all-out dream machine designed by the Gaylord brothers with Brooks Stevens, this car featured Chrysler or Cadillac power and a wild body by Spohn of Germany. The Gaylord also had a retractable hardtop and a spare tire tray that disappeared into the stern. Prices ranged up to $17,500, but production complications killed the car before initial orders were filled.

Grantham, 1954. Hollywood, California. Sports car kits for 110-inch wheelbases. The bodies were fiberglass.

Gregory, 1952. Kansas City, Missouri. The third car-making attempt by Ben Gregory, this was an 80-inch-wheelbase sports car with Porsche 1600cc engine.

Jomar, 1955. Saidel Sports Racing Cars. Manchester, New Hampshire. Design and chassis construction by TVR of England, with Saidel's own fiberglass body. Production ended in 1960, but the name appeared on some later imported TVRs.

Grantham of 1956, a fiberglass kit car.

Kurtis, built in 1949 by Kurtis-Kraft.

Keen Steam, 1958. Madison, Wisconsin. Also called the Streamliner. Steam-powered vehicles, later taken over by Williams.

King Midget, 1946. Midget Motors, Athens, Ohio. In continuous production through 1969, this was the most successful small runabout. Early cars were available only in kit form. New designs in 1951 resembled Jeeps, carried two passengers instead of one. The final, updated design, which even included tailfins, went into production in 1958. One-cylinder Wisconsin engines were used until 1966, when they were replaced by Kohler engines with higher horsepower. Wheelbases ranged from 72 to 76.5 inches; prices from $350 to $1000.

Kurtis, 1949. Kurtis-Kraft Inc., Glendale, California. Convertibles built by Frank Kurtis, first in 1949, after which he sold out to Muntz. In 1953, Kurtis resumed production. Two-seat sports cars were again offered, but 1953-55 Kurtis cars used Indy race-car styling. Any engine was available and some kit chassis were offered. In all, 21 assembled cars were built.

Maneco, 1954. Newport Beach, California. Frames, chassis and some complete cars were built for competition.

Martin Stationette, 1954. Commonwealth Research Corp. New York, New York. Three-wheeled tear-drop fiberglass body powered by 24-hp Hercules engine.

Maverick, 1953. Mountain View, California. A large, fiberglass three-passenger car using Cadillac chassis and drive train, plastic upholstery, marine plywood floor. Seven cars were built through 1955.

Moss, 1957. Inglewood, California. Small midget racing cars with fiberglass bodies and McCulloch chain-saw engines, priced at $595 for half-midget model.

Mota, 1953. Banning Electric, New York, New York. A gas-electric car with a fiberglass body.

Multiplex, 1952. Berwick, Pennsylvania. This firm made its first Multiplex in 1912-14: The '52 model was a two-seater made of production components, mainly from Studebaker and Willys. Three were built.

Muntz, 1950. Glendale, California and Evansville, Indiana. Based on the first, envelope-bodied Kurtis and sold by Earl "Mad Man" Muntz, the legendary TV maker. Muntz bought out Kurtis, built 28 cars in California and then moved to Evansville. Muntz Jets were similar to preceding Kurtis cars, but used only Cadillac engines. The Illinois cars were 16 inches longer and held four passengers instead of two. Later, Lincoln engines were used and the first aluminum bodies were replaced by steel. The Muntz Jet sold for over $5200 and would exceed 120 mph. Only 394 were produced, so the project did not make a profit.

Navajo, 1953. New York, New York. A 116-inch-wheelbase sports car "for the family" with Mercury V8 engine and Jaguar-like styling. The Navajo weighed 2300 pounds and sold for $2895. Production ended in 1954 or 1955.

Panda, 1955. Small Cars Inc., Kansas City, Missouri. Priced at $1000, this 70-inch-wheelbase shopper used either an Aerojet four-cylinder engine or a flat-twin Kohler.

Paxton, 1952. Los Angeles, California. Styled by Brooks Stevens. Only one prototype was built.

Pioneer, 1959. Nic-L-Silver Battery Co., Santa Ana, California. Electrics with two motors driving the rear wheels and a range of 40 to 100 miles. Fiberglass coupes, hardtops and wagons were offered, weighing 1800 pounds.

Plastic Atom, 1955. Sometimes called Atom, maker

unknown. Three-passenger plastic body with rear engine. Price: $1000.

Playboy, 1946. Buffalo, New York. Still selling, barely, in the 1950s, these were small economy cars with a 90-inch wheelbase. Most used Hercules four-cylinder engines. The body was of unit construction. A three-passenger convertible was priced at $985. Total production was between 90 and 97 units.

Powell, 1954. Compton, California. Metal and fiberglass pickup and some station wagon models built into 1956, selling for just over $1000.

Rambler 1902 Replica, 1959. American Air Products, Fort Lauderdale, Florida; later Gaslight Motors, Lathrup Village, Michigan.

Rogue, 1954. Origin unknown. Fiberglass sports body with 24-hp rear-mounted engine.

Scarab, 1958. Reventlow Automobiles Inc., Los Angeles, California. Competition cars using production components like the 1958 Corvette engine, tuned to produce 385 hp and 161 mph. Several models were built. Some of them were impressive competitors, but smaller displacement limits in European racing helped put an end to the project around 1963.

Scoot-Mobile, 1952. Norman Anderson, Owosso, Michigan. Three-wheeler with 12-hp two-cycle rear engine and roadster body, 108 inches in length.

Skorpion, 1952. Wilro Company, Pasadena, California. A small, good-looking fiberglass sports car priced at $445. It was mainly adaptable to the Crosley's chassis, but also used on the Ford's.

Skyline, 1953. Jamaica, New York. Two-seater based on Henry J, using the 85-hp Henry J/Willys Six. Many safety features including console controls, seat belts, high-back seats and padded dash were included. The price was less than $3000.

Star Dust, 1953. Los Angeles, California. Fiberglass sports car similar to Kaiser's Darrin.

Starlite, 1959. Kish Industries, Lansing, Michigan. Electric sports car priced at $3000, available as a convertible or hardtop with clear plastic roof.

Storm, 1954. Sports Car Development Corporation, Detroit, Michigan. A two-passenger Bertone-designed sports car, using a 250-hp Dodge V8.

Studillac, 1953. Bill Frick Motors, Rockville Centre, New York. Studebaker hardtops with Cadillac V8 engines. Top speed was 125 mph. The price was $1500 plus the cost of the Studebaker. Company also built Frick cars.

Sunmobile, 1955. General Motors, Detroit, Michigan. Experimental GM electric using photoelectric cells on its roof to power an electric motor.

Thrif-T, 1955. Tri-Wheel Motor Corp., Springfield, Massachusetts. An 85-inch wheelbase three-

Skorpion built in '52 for Crosley, Ford chassis.

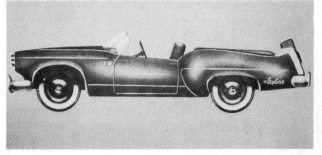

1953 Skyline, two-seater based on Henry J.

wheeler using a 10-hp flat-twin Onan engine. A five-passenger convertible and some trucks were built.

Tri-Car, 1955. Williamsport or Wheatland, Pennsylvania. A three-passenger, three-wheel fiberglass runabout powered by a Lycoming vertical twin engine, capable of 65 mph.

U.S. Mark II, 1956. U.S. Fiberglass Co., Norwood, New Jersey. Fiberglass convertible, with a wheelbase of 110 to 118 inches, available in kit form or assembled.

Victress, 1953. North Hollywood, California. Fiberglass kit car for 1940-48 Ford, Chevrolet and Plymouth chassis, priced at $695 to 795. A Victress did 208.105 mph at Bonneville in 1953.

Williams, 1957. Ambler, Pennsylvania. Production cars converted to steam power, built through 1968. In 1957, a Williams conversion sold for $7000.

Woodill, 1952. Willys and Dodge dealer Woody Woodill used a Glasspar body and Willys 90-hp chassis for his Wildfire series of two-seaters. Between 100 and 300 were built. Most of the cars were sold in kit form. A children's version was called Brushfire. Production continued into 1957 or 1958.

Yank, 1950. Custom Auto Works, San Diego, California. A two-seat, aluminum-body sports car powered by a Willys four-cylinder engine. Top speed was 78 mph; wheelbase was 100 inches; price was $1000.

Model Year Production Chart

Automotive production figures can be confusing, because car makers and industry observers sometimes discuss production in terms of model years and calendar years. The two are not the same: each firm builds cars of two different model years between January 1 and December 31 of a single calendar year.

The following chart lists production figures for model years rather than calendar years unless otherwise specified. (Most of the figures discussed in the text of CARS OF THE '50s are calendar-year figures.)

	1950	1951	1952	1953	1954	1955	1956	1957	1958	1959
Allstate			1,566	797						
Buick										
Special	337,909	164,448	120,153	217,170	190,884	381,249	334,017	220,242	139,213	
Century					81,982	158,796	102,189	65,966	37,568	
Super	195,853	169,226	135,332	190,514	118,630	132,463	80,988	70,250	42,388	
Roadmaster	78,034	66,058	46,217	77,438	50,571	64,527	53,427	47,582	14,054	
Skylark				1,690	836					
Limited									7,436	
LeSabre										164,904
Invicta										52,851
Electra										44,1185
Electra 225										22,308
Cadillac										
Sixty-One	26,772	4,700								
Sixty-Two	59,818	81,844	70,255	84,914	75,195	114,636	127,452	114,472	103,456	124,126
Sixty-Special	13,755	18,631	16,110	20,000	16,200	18,300	17,000	24,000	12,900	12,250
Seventy-Five	3,512	5,165	3,894	4,205	3,135	2,816	4,075	4,069	3,447	3,502
Eldorado				532	2,150	3,950	6,050	3,900	1,671	2,295
Eldorado Brougham								400	304	99
Chevrolet										
Special	284,857	205,907	118,681							
Deluxe	1,236,778	1,044,896	708,636							
150 & Delray				192,104	137,714	134,257	157,686	153,353	178,000*	
210 & Biscayne				649,821	524,222	805,309	737,371	653,358	377,000*	311,800*
Bel Air				514,760	486,240	773,238	540,682	702,220	532,000*	447,100*
Impala									60,000*	473,000*
Station Wagon									187,063	209,383
Corvette				315	3,640	674	3,388	6,246	9,168	9,670
Chrysler										
Royal	19,076									
Windsor	77,291		25,600§	32,192			86,080	48,055	26,975	35,473
Windsor DeLuxe			100,000§	52,277	44,527	98,874				
Saratoga	2,275		35,516§					37,196	18,476	17,479
New Yorker	24,441		52,200§	49,313	20,419		41,140	34,620	17,411	16,329
New Yorker DeLuxe				27,205	34,278	52,181				
300						1,725	1,102	2,402	809	690

* = approximate   § *Combined 1951 and 1952 production figures.*

	1950	1951	1952	1953	1954	1955	1956	1957	1958	1959
Chrysler										
Imperial	50		27,000§	8,859	5,661					
Crown Imperial	85		700§	160	100					
Town & Country	700									
Continental										
Mark II							1,325	444		
Mark III									12,550	
Mark IV										11,126
Clipper										
DeLuxe							5,715			
Super							9,172			
Custom							3,595			
Crosley										
Convertible	478	391	146							
Hot Shot/SS	742	646	358							
Sedan	1,367	1,077	216							
Station Wagon	4,205	4,500	1,355							
Cunningham										
C-2R		3								
C-3				15	3	2				
C-4R				3						
De Soto										
DeLuxe	35,678		25,199§							
Custom	100,525		123,000§							
Powermaster				45,602	21,204					
FireDome			45,800§	86,502	57,376	77,760	77,905	45,865	17,479	15,076
FireFlite						37,725	31,734	28,430	12,120	9,814
Adventurer							n.a.	1,950	432	699
FireSweep								41,369	19,414	20,844
Dodge										
Wayfarer	75,403		78,404§							
Coronet-Meadowbrook	267,694		417,605§	120,924						
Meadowbrook				15,751	15,444					
Coronet				156,498	74,401	110,972	142,613	160,979	77,388	96,782
Royal					69,803	76,660	48,780	40,999	15,165	14,807
Custom Royal						89,304	49,293	55,149	23,949	21,206
Station Wagon								30,481	20,196	23,590
Regal									1,163	
Edsel										
Ranger									24,049	28,418
Pacer									21,292	
Corsair									9,192	8,653
Citation									8,577	
Station Wagon										7,820
Ford										
Deluxe	388,368	220,618								
Custom	821,181	792,763						548,012	340,871	482,210
Mainline			163,911	305,714	233,680	127,301	164,442			
Customline			402,542	761,664	674,295	471,992	368,653			
Crestline			105,280	180,164	167,967					
Fairlane						626,250	645,306	785,886	424,569	178,800
Station Wagon						209,459	214,446	321,170	184,613	269,338
Thunderbird						16,155	15,631	21,380	37,892	67,456
Galaxie										464,336

§ *Combined 1951 and 1952 production figures.*

	1950	1951	1952	1953	1954	1955	1956	1957	1958	1959
Frazer										
Standard	2,200*	9,931								
Manhattan	1,500*	283								
Henry J										
4-cyl		38,500*	7,600*	8,500*	800*					
6-cyl		43,442*	8,951*	8,172*	323*					
Vagabond			7,017							
Hudson										
Pacemaker	61,752	34,495	7,486							
Super Six	17,246	22,532								
Super Eight	1,074									
Commodore Six	24,605	16,979	1,592							
Commodore Eight	16,731	14,243	3,125							
Hornet		43,666	35,921	27,208	24,833	13,130	6,395	3,876		
Wasp			21,876	17,792	11,603	7,191	2,519			
Jet				21,143	14,224					
Italia					9	16				
Rambler						25,214	5,000*			
Hornet Special							1,757			
Imperial										
(Standard)						11,260	10,458	18,066	7,063	
Crown Imperial						172	226	36	31	7
LeBaron								2,640	1,039	1,132
Crown								16,851	8,000	8,332
Custom										7,798
Kaiser										
Special	7,500*	60,000*			4,500*					
Deluxe	7,000*	80,000*	7,500*	8,000*						
Virginian			5,579							
Manhattan			19,000*	18,000*	4,110	1,291				
Carolina				1,812						
Dragon				1,277						
Darrin					435					
Lincoln										
(Standard)	17,489	16,761								
Cosmopolitan	10,701	15,813	20,399	14,122	7,441					
Capri			6,872	26,640	29,552	23,673	8,791	5,900	6,859	7,829
Premiere							41,531	35,223	10,275	7,851
Custom						3,549				
Mercury										
(Standard) Custom }	293,658	310,387	172,087	49,158	85,057	73,688	85,328			
Monterey }				256,705	174,238	151,453	105,369	157,528	62,312	89,277
Montclair						109,667	91,434	75,762	14,266	23,602
Medalist							45,812		18,732	
Turnpike Cruiser								16,861	6,407	
Station Wagon								36,012	22,302	24,598
Park Lane									9,252	12,523
Nash										
Statesman-Ambassador	145,782	125,203	99,086	89,100	41,653	37,298	14,352	5,000*		
Rambler	26,000	80,000	55,055	31,788	36,231	83,852	10,000*			
Nash-Healey		104	150	162	75*	15*				
Nash Metropolitan										
(shipments from UK)				743	13,162	6,096	9,068	15,317	13,128	22,309

* = approximate

	1950	1951	1952	1953	1954	1955	1956	1957	1958	1959
Oldsmobile										
76	33,426									
88	268,412	36,640	18,617	32,800	72,861	222,361	216,020	172,659	146,567	194,103
Super 88		150,457	118,558	201,334	187,816	242,193	179,000	132,039	88,992	107,660
98	106,222	100,519	76,245	99,872	93,325	118,627	90,439	79,694	60,816	81,102
Fiesta				458						
Packard										
Std-Super-Custom	46,650									
200/Clipper		71,362	54,000*	63,882	23,073	38,624		4,809		
250/Mayfair, Conv.		4,640	5,201	6,668	2,052					
300/Cavalier		15,309	6,705	10,799	2,580					
400/Patrician		9,001	3,975	7,481	2,760	16,333	6,999			
Caribbean				750	400	500	539			
Executive, Corp.				150	100		2,779			
Hawk									588	
Other									2,034	
Plymouth†										
DeLuxe	260,664									
Special DeLuxe	350,290									
Concord			139,914§							
Cambridge			281,201§	201,955						
Cranbrook			586,547§	445,496						
Plaza					113,266	153,182	130,817	142,371	124,888	
Savoy					199,517	108,738	268,982	108,437	171,907	182,465
Belvedere				3,000	150,365	139,155	436,259	272,765	140,701	169,910
Fury							4,500	7,438	5,303	81,830
Sport Fury										23,857
Pontiac										
Six/Chieftain 6	115,512	53,748	19,809	38,914	22,670					
Eight/Chieftain 8	330,887	316,411	251,564	379,705	149,986					
Chieftain						350,704	278,104	227,075	128,819	
Catalina										231,561
Super Chief									27,128	
Star Chief					115,088	203,104	127,325	105,768	48,795	68,815
Bonneville								630	12,240	82,564
Rambler										
(Registrations)							70,867	91,469	186,227	363,372
Studebaker (U.S.)										
Coupe, 3 pass.	4,457	3,730								
Coupe, 5 pass.	61,431	43,400	20,552	42,673	15,608	20,813				
Sedan, 2 dr	91,287	48,252	28,621	15,575	8,564	17,430	12,981	9,421	6,473	31,336
Sedan, 4 dr	152,082	142,786	90,792	63,615	26,243	57,391	34,019	26,887	18,850	48,459
Convertible	11,627	8,027	3,011							
Hardtop			24,686	29,713	7,642	9,964			3,009	14,235
Wagon, 2 dr					10,651	10,735	6,892	5,062	7,318	25,474
Wagon, 4 dr								5,142	2,330	
Golden Hawk							3,779	4,131	756	
Other Hawk							11,922	12,458	6,023	6,649
Willys										
Aero-Wing/Falcon			12,819	6,171						
Aero-Lark			7,474	16,405	5,003					
Aero-Ace			8,706	12,463	5,287	663				
Aero-Eagle			2,364	7,018	1,566					
Custom						3,686				
Bermuda						2,215				

†Plymouth 1957-59 figures include Canadian-built Plymouth-bodied variants, the De Soto Diplomat; the Dodge Regent, Kingsway, Crusader, Mayfair, Viscount.   * = approximate
§Combined 1951 and 1952 production figures.

Sources

The following list of books is intended as a source of further information about the makes of cars discussed in CARS OF THE '50s. Those under the heading "General History" and the brand names of cars deal with the history of 1950s automobiles. Books listed under the heading "Clubs and Vendors" contain information about car clubs, plus companies that sell special products or specific makes and models of cars.

General History
Georgano, G.N. *The Complete Encyclopedia of Motorcars.* Classic Motorbooks, P.O. Box 2, Osceola, WI 54020.

Allstate
See Kaiser

Buick
Dunne, Jim; Norbye, Jan P. *Buick: The Postwar Years.* Classic Motorbooks, P.O. Box 2, Osceola, WI 54020.

Cadillac
Hendry, Maurice D. *Cadillac: The Complete History.* Automobile Quarterly Publications, 245 W. Main St., Kutztown, PA 19530.

Chevrolet
Chappel, Pat. *The Hot One: Chevrolet 1955-1957.* Dragonwyck Publishing, Burrage Road, Contoocook, NH 02339.

Dammann, George H. *Sixty Years of Chevrolet.* Crestline Publishing, P.O. Box 48, Glen Ellyn, IL 60137.

Ludvigsen, Karl. *Corvette: America's Star-Spangled Sports Car.* Automobile Quarterly Publications, 245 W. Main St., Kutztown, PA 19530.

Chrysler
Langworth, Richard M. *Chrysler: The Postwar Years.* Dragonwyck Publishing, Burrage Road, Contoocook, NH 03229.

Continental
Ritch, Ocee. *The Lincoln Continental.* Classic Motorbooks, P.O. Box 2, Osceola, WI 54020.

Clipper
See Packard

De Soto
See Plymouth

Dodge
MacPherson, Thomas A. *The Dodge Story.* Crest-line Publishing, P.O. Box 48, Glen Ellyn, IL 60137.

Edsel
Deutsch, Jan G. *Selling the People's Cadillac.* Classic Motorbooks, P.O. Box 2, Osceola, WI 54020.

Ford
Dammann, George H. *Illustrated History of Ford.* Crestline Publishing, P.O. Box 48, Glen Ellyn, IL 60137.

"Ford Road" series on Thunderbird and 1950s Fords, Classic Motorbooks, P.O. Box 2, Osceola, WI 54020.

Henry J.
See Kaiser

Hudson
Langworth, Richard M. *Hudson: The Postwar Years.* Dragonwyck Publishing, Burrage Road, Contoocook, NH 03229.

Imperial
See Chrysler

Kaiser-Frazer
Langworth, R.M. *Kaiser-Frazer: Last Onslaught on Detroit.* Dragonwyck Publishing, Burrage Road. Contoocook, NH 03229.

Nash
Automobile Quarterly; Volume XV, Number 2. "Charles Nash and Nash Cars." Automobile Quarterly Publications, 245 W. Main St., Kutztown, PA 19530.

Packard
Dawes, Nathanial T. *The Packard 1942-1962.* Classic Motorbooks, P.O. Box 2, Osceola, WI 54020.

Plymouth
Butler, Don. *Fifty Years of De Soto-Plymouth.* Crestline Publishing, P.O. Box 48, Glen Ellyn, IL 60137.

Studebaker
Langworth, Richard M. *Studebaker: The Postwar Years.* Classic Motorbooks, P.O. Box 2, Osceola, WI 54020.

Willys
See Kaiser

Clubs and Vendors

Hirsch, John. *The Super Catalog of Car Parts and Accessories.* Classic Motorbooks, P.O. Box 2, Osceola, WI 54020.

Vintage Auto Almanac. Hemmings Motor News, P.O. Box 945, Bennington, VT 05201.